Praise for *Secrets from a Caterer's Kitchen*
BY NICOLE ALONI

"The chapter called '**What every caterer knows**' and the detailed food-quantity and beverage service charts make it **invaluable**." —*Bon Appétit*

"Aloni's book is funny, practical and creative . . . the **bible on entertaining**. All 150 recipes sound divine." —*Decor & Style Magazine*

"A clear and spirited guide . . . with easy, **surefire** recipes. **A lifesaver for the novice**, practical for even the most experienced party-giver." —*Publishers Weekly*

Cooking for Company

ALL THE RECIPES YOU NEED FOR SIMPLE,
ELEGANT ENTERTAINING AT HOME

Nicole Aloni

HPBooks

NOTICE: The information in this book is true and complete to the best of our knowledge. All recommendations on parts and procedures are made without any guarantees on the part of the author or publisher. The author and publisher disclaim all liability incurred in connection with the use of this information.

HPBooks
Published by The Berkley Publishing Group
A division of Penguin Group (USA) Inc.
375 Hudson Street
New York, New York 10014

Copyright © 2003 by Nicole Aloni
Text design by Richard Oriolo
Cover design by Jill Boltin
Cover illustrations by Gary Hovland

FIRST EDITION: September 2003

LIBRARY OF CONGRESS CATALOGING-IN-PUBLICATION DATA

Aloni, Nicole.
    Cooking for company : all the recipes you need for simple elegant entertaining at home / Nicole Aloni.—1st ed.
        p.   cm.
    Includes index.
    ISBN 1-55788-402-1
    1. Entertaining.   2. Cookery.   I. Title.

TX731.A613   2003
642'.4—dc21

2002192188

PRINTED IN THE UNITED STATES OF AMERICA

10 9 8 7 6 5 4 3 2 1

Acknowledgments

AGAIN, THE FATES PROVIDED ME with just the gifted eyes and voices I most needed to help me bring this concept to life. Many thanks to my support team mentioned below and to my students who have taught me.

Suzanne Schmalzer has commiserated and collaborated with me from the inception of this book as a proposal. A gifted writer herself, Suzanne has qualities cherished by an anxious author: clarity of vision and a razor-sharp editorial pencil. And patience. She was there for me when my focus strayed or my energy flagged. Suzanne also contributed insightful sidebars, recipe testing, wine recommendations and an introduction to her groovy husband, wine savant and contributor Peter Schmalzer.

Christy Hedges came to my kitchen fairly late in the project, but her skillful recipe testing, crystal clear writing and research put the wind under my wings to make the last miles feel like a fresh beginning. Evan Lewis returned to the kitchen for this book to lend her adventurous taste buds and enthusiasm. She always thinks outside the box, and her cocktails rock! Rose Garro and Sharon Vasak completed my good-hearted, talented treasure of a kitchen team. One and all the kind of people who make you look forward to a day of work.

I also got wonderful support from an ad hoc recipe testing/opinion panel I organized from willing friends. They double-checked recipes and kept me in touch with how real people really cook. This valuable group included Tiffany Atkinson, Wil Brown, Sandi Cottrell, Sandi Flanigan, Vivian Levin, Leslie Marcus, Jan and Bruce Macdonald, Leeann Richards, Suzanne Schmalzer, Candy Wallace and Ruth Webster.

My editor was once again the clear-sighted, knowledgeable and supportive Jeanette Egan. It was a pleasure to work on a book about entertaining with someone who is a great entertainer and cook in her own right. Gary Hovland also returned to provide the captivating illustrations. His charming, lighthearted style perfectly expresses my approach to hospitality: Don't worry. Be happy.

I am fortunate to continue to be guided by my agent, Jane Dystel. She leads the way and watches my back (a contortionist's job if ever there was one).

Finally, Aminadav. You were and are my inspiration to pursue the best in myself.

Contents

Preface

Part of the secret of success in life is to eat what you want and let the food fight it out inside.

—Mark Twain

"PSSST. EXCUSE ME. CAN YOU help me? I know I should be able to handle this, but I just don't know where to begin. I want to have some friends over for a dinner party. It's very important that I do this well, and I'm afraid I'll make a fool of myself. I know other people do it all the time; I just don't know how they have the nerve. This is so embarrassing. As a professional, do you have any advice?" In the course of teaching cooking and entertaining across America, I've heard that furtive confession over and over. I've talked with hundreds of people about their entertaining expectations. I've huddled at the back of the classroom with editors, doctors, chefs, lawyers and even a psychic to talk about what made their party-giving stressful or successful.

I was shocked by their unanimous response. These dissimilar people all had the same concerns. A chorus of voices wailed, "I love to entertain, but I don't have the time to prepare the kind of food I would like to serve." Even the psychic hadn't divined her answer to comfortable entertaining.

I realized my students needed a book I knew how to write—a guide focused on a short list of essential entertaining recipes, each of which met my caterer's criteria for surefire party food: easy, done ahead, delicious and beautiful. These recipes, plus some simple tips about setting up the party, would ensure that everyone who owned this book could finally learn to entertain with confidence. Cheers!

Introduction

One cannot think well, love well, sleep well, if one has not dined well.

—Virginia Woolf

We may live without poetry, music and art;
We may live without conscience, and live without heart;
We may live without friends; we may live without books;
But civilized man cannot live without cooks.

—Owen Meredith

EVERYONE I KNOW LIKES THE *idea* of giving a party, but about 98 percent of them find it more stressful than gratifying to carry out. Generations of two-career families have contributed to a society in which the opportunity to learn about cooking and entertaining in the stress-free environment of your childhood kitchen is a rarity. My cooking school students, friends and clients tell me they would like to entertain, and then recite a grocery list of reasons not to: they don't have all of the perfect dishes, glasses, linens or napkin rings; they lack confidence in their cooking skills; their dining table is too small and their anxiety is too big. They postpone one opportunity to celebrate after another.

Here's my plan: In *Cooking for Company*, I will stand beside you in your kitchen as you learn the recipes I can't live without when I entertain. They are the easy-to-make, easy-to-shop for essentials of my menus. *Cooking for Company* shows you how to build a foundation for confident hospitality.

To guide you in the process of making entertaining an everyday experience, I have ruthlessly eliminated every recipe that is nonessential. The modest number of master recipes that remain have passed the most stringent screening. Gone are recipes that require an aebleskiver pan or handwoven baking basket. Recipes that demand your presence in the kitchen while your guests are enjoying themselves in the dining room are history. Instead, the recipes in this book are for dishes that:

- **Are delicious, attractive and easy to prepare, yet look like they took all day.**

- **Have flavors that represent *safe adventure*—traditional enough to appeal to your grandmother's palate, yet sophisticated enough to impress your new fashion designer daughter-in-law.**

- **Are prepared with only ingredients that can be found at a local well-stocked supermarket rather than at some expensive gourmet store (food church) all the way across town.**

- **Can be prepared hours, days or weeks in advance.**

- **Represent a comprehensive collection that provides a solution to what to serve for every type of social occasion at every season.**

I made it my goal, as I created these delicious recipes, to anticipate and eliminate every challenge you might encounter from stovetop to tabletop. Sometimes that meant not including a delicious, tested recipe that just took too much time to prepare. I also made it my goal to provide two or three simple variations to each of these fifty-five master recipes. Once you have prepared the original, the variations expand your menu options without requiring you to think through a new recipe or buy new equipment. To entertain beautifully you need only master seven or eight of these great recipes each year.

The occasions that cause you to fret are usually stressful because of the special guests invited. Well, those luminaries are undoubtedly not coming to your home more than three or four times in a year. If you have a couple of entrées, a great salad dressing, two dramatic desserts and some seasonal vegetable yummies under your apron, you've got plenty of options to create four or five successful menus and a year of low-stress, impressive entertaining!

To begin, select a small number of recipes at which you can become fearlessly adept. To assist you in recipe selection and menu planning there are some short descriptions at the top of each recipe. Use these as a quick way to ensure that each recipe meets your needs for the occasion.

Recipe Characteristics

- **Kid appeal**
- **Good for a casual occasion**
- **Good for a formal affair**
- **Good on a buffet**
- **Good for a picnic**
- **Vegetarian option**
- **Healthy**
- **Quick and easy**
- **Inexpensive**
- **Pricey**
- **Completed in advance (totally)**

These recipes will form the framework on which you can build a repertoire of your own specialties. For complete peace of mind you need to prepare the recipes once or twice before the party so you can work out the kinks your home will add. You'll need time to adjust for the fact that your kids have broken the kitchen timer and the dog ran off with the beater for your mixer.

Once you have mastered a selection of these recipes that you find appealing, you can confidently add in a trendy new dish clipped out of a magazine or downloaded from the Food Network's website. And good news: mixing in a purchased delicacy or two is recommended. My entertaining mantra: "Do what you do best, and buy the rest."

To ensure successful planning, every recipe includes two very important features. First, beverage pairings are suggested (often wine) that complement the food. And, to assist you in making the presentation of your dishes more manageable, every recipe includes recommended serving utensils and equipment. Once you have selected a recipe, while you accumulate your grocery shopping list, including the recommended beverages, you should also create a separate list for supplies. With these two lists completed you will have a master plan for everything you need to wash, buy, borrow or rent. There's no sense in preparing a masterful whole roast fish (see chart, page 123) only to discover you don't have a platter big enough to hold it.

More good news: you do not need dozens of hollyhock napkin rings or a sterling silver ice bucket and tongs to entertain with panache. What you do need are some key pieces of equipment and multipurpose serving pieces. Following is the list of what I use for successful entertaining.

Entertaining Essentials

- Electric hot tray

- 4- to 8-quart chafing dish

- Serving tongs (long and short)

- Cake stand (This is multipurpose: use it for a cake, any special dessert, hors d'oeuvres, tarts, Brie en croûte. It adds height and visual interest to your buffet table.)

- Multiple beverage cooler (bucket or tub)

- Cheese board (It can be made of wood, marble, slate or granite. Invest in something you love, as you will use it forever.)

- Cheese knives to go with the board

- Large, soft-sided insulated cooler—the *real* picnic basket

- Large bowl for pasta or salad

- Soup tureen with candle or other heating element (It should be nice enough to put on the table to use for soup, chili, stroganoff or pasta.)

- Several beautiful serving platters (They should be 16 to 24 inches and round, octagonal, rectangular or square. They should be handsome enough that you don't need to add any time-consuming garnish for the presentation to look finished. At least one should be deep for serving saucy entrées like curry on a bed of rice.)

Roasting Charts

Important reference tools are provided for you with the inclusion of roasting charts for beef, pork, lamb, poultry and fish on pages 120 to 126. For many of the most formal menus (pages 203 to 217), the entrée is based on a simply elegant cut of roast meat or fish. These charts tell you how much to serve each person, how long to cook it, how to know when it's done and advises you about complementary spices and herbs.

Menus

Cooking for Company is completed with suggested party menus for different seasons and popular occasions, from a summer picnic to a winter buffet lunch plus all the major holidays. These menus are a practical combination of the recipes in the book and complementary dishes you can purchase in most grocery store delis. Good food is only a great menu when it's combined properly. Suggested beverages (wine or cocktails and nonalcoholic choices) are also selected for each menu.

Techniques

In order to satisfy your desire for great food accomplished simply, some specific cooking procedures are excluded from the book. There are no pastry recipes beyond pie crust and cookie dough. No recipe requires the cook to butcher or fillet any meat or seafood. Any decent grocery employs someone who already knows eye of round from eye of newt. In acknowledgment of the growing number of vegetarians, there are also numerous vegetarian options in all the recipe categories.

Pantry

A well-stocked pantry is an entertaining necessity especially for unexpected company. Ready-to-open, flavorful sauces, garnishes, dips, snacks and hors d'oeuvres are your party magic kit. Many of the items I rely on can be found in your supermarket. However, some of these flavorful, often ethnic, ingredients are only found in gourmet or specialty stores and are well worth adding to your pantry as you become more adventurous.

Pantry Necessities from the Supermarket
- **Pickled foods: capers, cornichons, cucumber pickles, watermelon pickles, baby corn, jalapeños en escabeche, stuffed grape leaves, many varieties of olives, mushrooms, hot yellow peppers, pepperoncini, hearts of palm**

- **Relishes: chutney, salsa, sweet corn relish, sun-dried tomatoes packed in olive oil**

- **Canned: coconut milk, garbanzo and cannellini beans, sardines, anchovies, clams, smoked oysters, green and chipotle chiles**

- **Frozen: peeled and deveined shrimp, puff pastry, pie crust sheets, homemade stock, hard cheeses, Brie, cream cheeses, sweet butter**

- **Dry: corn chips, a variety of crackers and crostini, Armenian flat bread, nuts (salted, roasted and caramelized), dried fruit, dried mushrooms, chile pods**

Have a Party

Cooking for Company is a lifeline extended to those of you who find yourselves over-worked and undersocialized, spending too much time dining in the car, communicating via cell phone and PDA, and too little time in your home. Strangers cook most of our meals while our kitchens languish and hospitality is as elusive as Mount Everest. Following is a road map to the top of the mountain where the table I've set is waiting for you and your company. Rest assured, your guests aren't looking for five-course meals served by a suave waiter and a wine steward. They're hungry for exactly what you have to offer, a chance to get to know you better and to enjoy the comforts of your home and the food you have prepared just for them. *Cooking for Company* will give you back to your guests. When that doorbell rings, you won't be called upon to do anything more complex than listen for the timer to beep or the champagne to pop.

Strange to see how a good dinner and feasting reconciles everybody.

—Samuel Pepys

Cooking for Company

Hors d'Oeuvres

Kissing don't last: cookery do!
—George Meredith

THE KIND OF HORS D'OEUVRES that have met my criteria for this book are reduced to what is essential: hors d'oeuvres that are delightful in their presentation, easy to eat and satisfying as an accompaniment to a cocktail or other cold drink. These recipes have been culled from the bright flavors and traditions of many cultures.

Ethnic markets, the prepared foods section of a good grocery store and some restaurants can also provide you with a variety of excellent hors d'oeuvres. For this reason, they are often included in the menu chapter, starting on page 203, as recommended purchases.

How Much to Serve

Whether it's for a few people or for thirty, plan a combination of by-the-piece items, like a filled polenta cup, and multiple-portion recipes, like Brie en croûte. The bulk dishes are always less time consuming to prepare. Also try to include at least one item that's vegetarian, to appeal to those looking for lighter fare and the ever-growing number of vegetarians. Balance this with something indulgent or rich.

The quantities for an hors d'oeuvres reception preceding dinner should be about half of what would be served if the party were hors d'oeuvres only. Time of day also has an impact on your quantities. If a cocktail party is called for 7 to 9 PM, your guests will rightly expect to be provided with enough food to replace their dinner. In general, the quantities that I recommend are:

- **Hors d'oeuvres preceding dinner: 5 to 7 bites per person**
- **Hors d'oeuvres for a cocktail party that doesn't include dinner: 7 to 9 bites per person**
- **Hors d'oeuvres as dinner: 12 to 14 bites per person**

Choosing a Theme

Choosing a theme for an hors d'oeuvre menu is particularly successful. It gives you a structure around which to plan the menu. Where you might find a three-course Indian or Caribbean menu hard to execute, hors d'oeuvres offer the same adventure in bite-size portions. One easy approach is to plan your menu around what you know is available at a favorite ethnic market complemented by two or three of your specialties.

Quick and Easy Hors d'Oeuvres

Since hors d'oeuvre parties often come together at the last minute, I am including a list of my quick-to-assemble favorites and pantry items that can practically be served as is.

Straight from the pantry quickies

These require little more than opening a container and combining with on-hand ingredients.

- Bar nuts (or the nuts on page 43)

- Olives (see box, page 44–45)

- Cheeses (see box, page 29–30), many can be stored in the freezer

- Pickled things (cornichons, baby corn, capers, mushrooms)

- Good-quality extra-virgin olive oil for dipping, balsamic vinegar

- Jarred goat or feta in oil (mix with fresh tomatoes for a relish)

- Stuffed grape leaves, caponata, cannellini, and black beans

- Lump crabmeat, smoked oysters, and Italian oil-packed tuna

- Salsa, chutney, sun-dried tomatoes, tahini

- Freshly purchased herbs and spices

- Pita chips, bread chips, assorted crackers, tiny toasts

I keep cream cheese in the freezer to serve as a base to create dips and spreads with bright additions like chopped imported olives, pesto or chopped sun-dried tomatoes and fresh basil. I also keep crostini (page 16) and great baguettes in the freezer to make toast points and bruschetta in a flash.

Quick to Prepare

These hors d'oeuvres may require some shopping but can be pulled together in less than 10 minutes:

- Disc of chevre rolled in herbs and wrapped in prosciutto, sautéed briefly in a hot pan.

- Spicy Tangerine Shrimp: Marinate 1 pound peeled, raw shrimp in half of the recipe for Evan's Tangerine Vinaigrette (page 135) for 20 minutes. Thread on skewers and grill until done, about 4 minutes. Mix remaining half of vinaigrette with 2 to 3 table-spoons orange marmalade and a pinch of red chile flakes and use as a dipping sauce for shrimp.

- Open-face sandwiches on tiny pumpernickel: smoked salmon, prosciutto or Parma ham with a slice of fig and a Parmesan curl; cucumber and salmon cream cheese; pâté and a slice of pear; rare roast beef, horseradish and a sliver of anchovy.

- Scallop Lettuce Tacos: Slice large scallops into thirds. Sauté in hot pan with unsalted butter 2 to 3 minutes until opaque. Cool and toss with Lavender Mayonnaise (page

140) or Rouille (page 140). Put in an endive spear or small lettuce leaf and decorate with chopped chives or caviar.

- Goat cheese mixed with blue cheese, ground shrimp or mushrooms to pipe or spread on endive leaves, cucumber discs or snow peas.

- Grilled Chile Chicken Wings: Clip the tips from the wings and cut apart at the joint. Marinate in the refrigerator for 8 hours (or longer) in the Honey-Ginger Asian Marinade (page 131). Pat dry and grill over medium-hot fire until done, 10 to 12 minutes. Serve with Avocoda-Chipotle Salsa (page 144) or purchased satay sauce.

- Shiitake Mushroom and Shrimp on Rosemary Skewers: Brush mushrooms and shrimp with herbed olive oil (rosemary, thyme, lemon) and grill.

- Halved fresh figs or apricots filled with a nub of blue cheese and pecans.

- Gruyère Walnut Crisps: Grate ½ pound of Gruyère or good Parmesan cheese and toss with 2 tablespoons minced fresh tarragon, rosemary or thyme. Make mounds of about 2 teaspoons of the cheese mixture on a sheet pan covered with parchment paper. Sprinkle mounds with toasted, chopped walnuts or almonds. Bake at 350°F (180°C) for about 8 minutes, until they've melted into golden wafers. Transfer to a rack to cool. Serve alone, or with a soup or salad.

- Skewers of fresh figs wrapped with bacon, brushed with balsamic vinegar and honey and broiled.

- Goat Cheese and Sun-Dried Tomato Pizzette: Cut good sourdough bread into ½-inch slices, brush with olive oil and toast in the oven. Top with a schmear of purchased tapenade or Arugula Pesto (page 138), a slice of goat cheese and a relish made from minced sun-dried tomatoes, minced basil, minced fresh tomato and a splash of balsamic vinegar. Bake about 5 minutes at 350°F (180°C). Serve with a sprinkle of fresh parsley.

- Skewers of thinly cut strips of chicken, beef or lamb brushed with oil or a vinaigrette and grilled to serve with any of the pestos (pages 136 to 138), a purchased satay sauce or plain yogurt mixed with mint and cumin.

- Almost a BLT: Crisply cook 3 to 4 slices of bacon. Pat dry and mince. Mix with ¾ cup mayonnaise (page 139), 1 teaspoon minced garlic and 2 teaspoons Dijon mustard. Spread generously on pumpernickel or rye bread. Top with a slice of perfectly ripe tomato and some chopped green onion. Press another bread slice with the bacon spread on top. Use a biscuit cutter or knife to trim into bite-size canapés.

- Deviled Eggs: Mix yolks with Mustard-Tarragon or Sesame-Ginger Mayonnaise (page 140). Top with a sprig of dill or cilantro, a little caviar or crumbled bacon.

- Feta and Honey Wheels: Slice mild feta very thin, pat dry and arrange on thinly sliced pumpernickel. Drizzle with a mixture of honey, minced rosemary and a generous amount of freshly ground coarse black pepper.

- Artisan sausages cut into discs, skewered, grilled and served with exotic mustards and a bowl of olives.

- Balsamic Cheese Nibbles: Cut Asiago or Parmigiano-Reggiano cheese into small cubes and drizzle with extra-fine balsamic vinegar. Toss and let rest 20 minutes. To serve, drizzle on a little more balsamic vinegar and sprinkle with minced pistachios and dried apricots or dates.

- Breadsticks wrapped with prosciutto served alongside melon wrapped with prosciutto.

Wine and Beverage Notes

Here are some beverage notes for pairing wine with hors d'oeuvres from my friend and wine expert Peter Schmalzer.

When choosing wines to accompany an array of different hors d'oeuvres, it's best to remember the principle called Occam's Razor, which states that for any given problem, all other things being equal, the simplest answer is usually the best one. The simplest answers here, I find, are aperitifs. Not exactly cocktails, and not really wines, either, aperitifs exist for the express purpose of sparking the appetite prior to the main event. Classic aperitifs balance a touch of sweetness with a pleasant bitter taste and seem to go with a wide range of appetizers. Lillet, with its orange/almond character, is especially satisfying served chilled with a twist. Others include the bitter cherry Campari, sweetish Dubonnet and, of course, dry, herbal French or Italian vermouth. If you wish to serve wine, however, the same idea applies: for both whites and reds, simple, straightforward and fruity wines like Sauvignon Blanc or Beaujolais lend themselves easily to hors d'oeuvres and set the stage for more serious wines to follow.

A special cocktail is one of the simplest ways to add flair to your party and can be managed by even the rawest recruit bartender. I have included a number of suggestions starting on page 191. When you are featuring a special drink, it is still a good idea to offer a wine and a nonalcoholic beverage such as mineral water, iced tea or sparkling cider.

Crab Cakes

Because these crab cakes are practically all crab, the quality of the crabmeat really shows. Therefore, they are only worth making if you use lump meat from the blue or Dungeness crab. For entertaining, I recommend baking rather than frying the crab cakes; they will stay fresh longer and are much cleaner to prepare and to eat. The original recipe has been adapted from my previous book, *Secrets from a Caterer's Kitchen*. The Thai variation is all-new and absolutely spectacular. The third variation, with bananas included in the Thai recipe, provides one of those flavor surprises I love to include in an entertaining menu.

Buffet • Formal • Pricey

PARTY TIME PREPARATIONS: Bake and serve.

SERVING EQUIPMENT: A large, flat tray or dish (ideally resting on a hot tray), small serving fork or spatula, small bowl for the sauce and cocktail napkins.

BEVERAGE TO ACCOMPANY: Fumé Blanc, dry Gewürztraminer

Makes 16 to 20 little cakes, 1½ cups sauce

HERB SAUCE
¾ cup mayonnaise
¼ cup sour cream
¼ cup chopped parsley
¼ cup chopped cilantro, chives or chervil
2 tablespoons minced shallot
2 tablespoons fresh lemon juice
2 tablespoons capers, drained
¼ teaspoon hot pepper sauce
¼ teaspoon each kosher salt and freshly ground coarse black pepper

CRAB CAKES
½ pound lump crabmeat
¼ cup minced scallions

¼ cup finely diced red bell pepper
1½ teaspoons minced fresh basil or cilantro
2 to 3 tablespoons mayonnaise
1¼ teaspoons fresh lemon juice
⅛ teaspoon dry mustard
⅛ teaspoon Dijon mustard
¾ tablespoon Old Bay seasoning
½ egg, slightly beaten
4 tablespoons panko or fine bread or cracker crumbs
Kosher salt and freshly ground coarse black pepper, to taste

1. **FOR THE SAUCE:** Put the mayonnaise, sour cream, parsley and cilantro into a food processor and pulse to blend. Stir in the remaining ingredients and taste for herbs, salt and pepper. Refrigerate until ready to use. This will keep well in the refrigerator for 3 to 4 days.

2. **FOR THE CRAB CAKES:** Pick through the crabmeat to remove any cartilage, being careful not to break down the chunks. Combine the crabmeat, all of the minced vegetables and the basil or cilantro in a large bowl.

3. In a second bowl, combine the mayonnaise, lemon juice, mustards and seasoning. Gently fold this into the crab mixture. Fold in the egg. Sprinkle in 2 tablespoons of the crumbs, salt and pepper and fold together, being careful to leave the crab chunks. You should have a moist, but manageable mixture. If it is too sloppy to form, add a little more crumbs.

4. Form into 16 to 20 bite-size cakes (about 1 inch in diameter). Press the remaining crumbs onto all sides of the cakes. Place on a flat tray, wrap and refrigerate for 1 hour to overnight before cooking.

5. Preheat the broiler. Place the cakes on a greased baking sheet. Broil for a total of 3 to 5 minutes, flipping once. They can then be held warm in the oven for up to 30 minutes. To serve, top each crab cake with a dollop of the sauce and an herb leaf.

❋ VARIATIONS

Thai Crab Cakes For the sauce, use cilantro in place of the parsley and chives (a total of ½ cup chopped cilantro).

In Step 2, replace half of the crab with 4 ounces lean ground pork and use both the minced basil and cilantro. In Step 3, eliminate the two mustards and Old Bay seasoning and add 1 tablespoon fish sauce, ⅛ teaspoon sugar, 1½ tablespoons minced fresh ginger, ¼ teaspoon cayenne pepper, 1 tablespoon minced garlic and 1 minced, seeded small serrano chile. Shape and cook as above.

Thai Banana Crab Cakes Add ⅓ cup mashed ripe banana to the Thai Crab Cakes in Step 2.

THE CRUDITÉ PRINCIPLE

Crudité: raw seasonal vegetables, often accompanied by a dipping sauce.
—Sharon Tyler Herbst, *Food Lover's Companion*

Fresh vegetables are a proven solution for menu-planning problems. Most people like them and you can be sure that anyone on a special diet can eat them. I cannot count the number of times I've been in line behind someone at a buffet who whispered, "Well at least I can eat the vegetables."

And there are many more reasons why a crisp basket or bowl of fresh vegetables appears at nearly every reception I've ever given. Their preparation is simple. They can be clustered to make a bright, colorful display, and their refreshing flavor and texture are a good counterpoint to richer dishes. I also appreciate them on my menu because they can be prepared well ahead of time, as can their complementary dips or fillings.

TIPS FOR A SUCCESSFUL DISPLAY

Only use vegetables that are in season and, if possible, grown locally. The beautiful and often exotic produce available in farmers markets and specialty grocers today are a welcome addition to a crudité. Because they are to be consumed in their most unadorned state, freshness will more than make up for any lack in variety.

Tartlets

Whether you make your own pie crust, using the recipe below, or purchase pie crust dough, these are great hors d'oeuvres. Made in mini muffin pans, they are just the right size. These savory shells can be baked ahead and frozen to pull out at a moment's notice. Fill them with everything from caponata to sautéed scallops and poblano chile or slivered sausage and grapes. If you use purchased pie crust, skip Steps 1 to 3 below.

Buffet • Formal • Vegetarian Option

PARTY TIME PREPARATION: Fill and/or bake and serve.

SERVING EQUIPMENT: A flat serving tray or basket and cocktail napkins.

BEVERAGE TO ACCOMPANY: Fumé Blanc, dry Gewürztraminer

Makes 48 tiny tartlets

PIE CRUST
2½ cups all-purpose flour
1 teaspoon salt

1 cup (2 sticks) cold butter, cut into bits
3 to 6 tablespoons ice water

1. Combine the flour and salt in a food processor. Pulse to mix. Add the butter and process in pulses until the largest pieces of butter are the size of a pea, about 10 seconds. With the machine running, add 3 tablespoons of cold water by drops just until the dough begins to pull together. Test the texture by squeezing some dough into a ball. If it is too crumbly to hold together, add a few more drops of water. Don't process for more than 30 seconds total time. (To make by hand, combine the flour and salt in a large bowl. Use two knives or a pastry cutter to work in the butter to the large crumb stage. Drip in the cold water until the dough comes together, but is not wet or sticky.) Transfer the dough to a sheet of plastic wrap. Flatten the dough into a disc, wrap well and refrigerate for 2 hours or overnight.

2. Remove the dough from the refrigerator and allow to stand at room temperature for 5 to 10 minutes, until it gives slightly when pressed. Put on a floured board or marble and, starting in the middle, roll the dough evenly in each direction. Flip, dust with flour and roll out to about ⅛-inch thickness. Cut the dough into 2-inch squares. Spray the muffin cups with vegetable oil spray. Arrange the squares into each cup, pressing down the bottoms to create a flat seat for the finished hors d'oeuvre. Cover with plastic wrap and chill for 1 hour.

3. Preheat the oven to 375°F (190°C). Prick the bottom of each shell and bake for about 15 minutes, until crisp and light gold. Cool completely on a rack before filling. The cups can be tightly wrapped at this stage and frozen for up to two weeks. To use, thaw in the refrigerator, then crisp briefly on a baking sheet in a 350°F (180°C) oven before filling.

4. The tartlets can be filled with a cold or warm filling. For a warm filling, heat the completed tart in a 350°F (180°) oven for 5 to 10 minutes before serving.

NOTE: When making pie crust, everything should be as cold as possible at each stage: the butter, water, food processor bowl and blade. The dough should be well chilled after each step of handling.

🌾 VARIATIONS

Room Temperature Fillings

- Sour cream or crème fraîche, caviar and a sprig of watercress
- Avocado-Chipotle Salsa (page 144) and a sliver of grilled or poached shrimp
- Chicken salad made with the Sesame-Ginger Mayonnaise (page 140)
- Smoked Trout Pâté (page 26), topped with chopped chives or pistachios
- Roquefort cheese, watercress and diced cucumber, garnished with a tarragon sprig

Warm Fillings

- Multitude of Mushrooms and Cream Sauce (page 117), topped with a thyme sprig
- Sliced fresh fig, crumbled goat cheese, minced candied ginger and a drizzle of honey
- Slivers of sautéed gourmet sausage, sliced seedless grapes and fontina cheese
- A dot of goat cheese and a drizzle of the Arugula Pesto (page 138)
- A sliver of sautéed foie gras, chopped fresh blueberries, a drizzle of balsamic vinegar and sprinkle of thyme

Stuffed Mushrooms

The mushroom is a culinary chameleon, sometimes in the forefront making a bold state-ment—think morel omelet or a grilled portobello sandwich—and other times blending in to bring harmony to other strong flavors as in the Cuban Flavored-Braised Beef Short Ribs (page 85). In the ubiquitous stuffed mushroom, the malleable fungus serves as the backdrop for a flavorful filling.

Now that exotic mushrooms are available with remarkable frequency in your grocery store, try using one of them to give this concept an updated style. The fillings included below can be used to fill a white button for a bite-size hors d'oeuvre, or a giant portobello or shiitake to serve as a first course or vegetarian entrée. If you are using white buttons, marinating them before stuffing improves the flavor and texture. If you are using the more flavorful portobello or shiitake, that step can be ignored.

Buffet • Quick and Easy • Vegetarian Option

PARTY TIME PREPARATION: Bake and serve

SERVING EQUIPMENT: A flat tray with a raised lip, small tongs or fork and cocktail napkins.

BEVERAGE TO ACCOMPANY: Alsatian Riesling, Gewürztraminer, Côte du Rhône

Makes 24 hors d'oeuvres

MUSHROOMS

24 (1- to 1½-inch) mushrooms (about 1½ pounds)

2 tablespoons olive oil

3 tablespoons fresh lemon juice or balsamic vinegar

Kosher salt and freshly ground coarse black pepper, to taste

BASIC FILLING

¼ cup unsalted butter

¼ cup minced shallots

¼ teaspoon kosher salt

2 tablespoons dry vermouth or Madeira

2 tablespoons minced thyme, parsley or basil

3 tablespoons cornbread or sourdough bread crumbs

2 tablespoons whipping cream or crème fraîche

3 tablespoons grated Asiago or Parmesan cheese

1. **TO PREPARE THE MUSHROOMS:** Brush the mushrooms with a damp cloth to clean. Remove the stems and use a melon baller or paring knife to scoop out enough flesh to create a generous cavity for the filling without leaving the mushroom too thin to hold up. Mince and reserve 1½ cups of the mushroom trimmings.

2. Toss the mushrooms with the olive oil, lemon juice and salt and pepper. Put in a

ABOUT MUSHROOMS

Mushrooms add earthy flavors to savory dishes. When selecting mushrooms at your grocery store, look for plump specimens. Choose mushrooms with smooth, rounded caps that fold over the gills at the base of the stem. Store them in a paper bag in the refrigerator; the paper draws moisture out of the spongy mushrooms, keeping them fresher longer. When you are ready to serve or cook with them, instead of washing them, use a brush or dry paper towel to remove any dirt from the skin.

In the grocery store you will typically find the following selections of both fresh and dried mushrooms.

FRESH, COMMONLY AVAILABLE MUSHROOMS

- White buttons: The most common; 1- to 3-inch caps; good sautéed, stuffed or in sauces
- Shiitakes: Medium brown in color; 2- to 5-inch caps; the stems should be discarded; unique, slightly garlicky taste; retain their shape even after long simmering; excellent in sauces, soups and stir-fries. Release less liquid when cooked than other fresh mushrooms.
- Creminis: Immature portobellos; more flavorful than white mushrooms; good sautéed, stuffed or in sauces
- Portobellos: 4- to 7-inch flat brown caps; tough stem; large size and meaty flavor make them perfect to grill or sauté, whole or sliced

resealable plastic bag and marinate at room temperature for 1 hour or for 3 to 4 hours in the refrigerator.

3. **TO MAKE THE FILLING:** Melt 2 tablespoons of the butter in a skillet over medium-high heat. Add the shallots and sauté until softened, about 2 minutes. Add the mushroom trimmings and salt and sauté until dry, 3 to 4 minutes. Add the vermouth and thyme and cook 2 minutes. Remove from the heat and let cool.

4. Add the crumbs, cream and cheese and toss to mix.

5. Fill each mushroom cap with a mounded ball of the filling. Melt the remaining butter and drizzle over the mushrooms. The mushrooms can be prepared up to this point and refrigerated for up to 4 hours before baking.

6. Preheat oven to 400°F (205°C). Bake on a baking sheet lined with parchment paper for 12 to 15 minutes, until bubbling and browned. Serve immediately or at room temperature.

- Porcinis: Large, puffy caps with stubby stems; intense, earthy, robust mushroom flavor; excellent in sauces or stews; meaty texture, especially if grilled

- Oysters: Translucent, white; very mild flavor; melt into a sauce or soup to lend mild mushroom notes

- Enokis: Tiny white threads with button tops; use raw or add to soups at last minute

LESS COMMON, (EXPENSIVE AND DELICIOUS) FRESH MUSHROOMS

- Morels: Pointed, honeycombed caps; beige to brown; nutty, woodsy flavor; wonderful in soups, omelets and game sauces

- Chanterelles: Gold or apricot colored; shaped like a trumpet; tiny to 6-inch size; peppery, nutty, cinnamonlike flavors; excellent with eggs, seafood and poultry

DRIED

Shiitakes, morels, chanterelles and porcinis are often available in dried form. Dried mushrooms are expensive, usually packaged in 1½- to 2-ounce packets that cost from $5 to $14. Because their flavor is concentrated, an ounce or even less will add robust flavor to an entrée for eight guests.

VARIATIONS

Bacon-Sage Stuffed Mushrooms In Step 4, also add 2 slices smoked bacon, cooked and crumbled, 2 tablespoons chèvre and 2 teaspoons minced fresh sage.

Crab-Stuffed Mushrooms In Step 4, also add ⅓ cup lump crabmeat, 1 teaspoon minced tarragon or basil, 1 tablespoon fresh lemon juice and 2 teaspoons grated lemon zest.

Brie- and Pecan–Stuffed Mushrooms In Step 4, delete the Asiago or Parmesan cheese and add ½ cup diced Brie, Teleme or Reblochon cheese, ¼ cup minced, dried apricots and ¼ cup chopped, toasted pecans.

Polenta Cups

The cornmeal and herbs in the dough for the Polenta Cups create a pretty hors d'oeuvre container with tons of flavor all on its own. The directions to prepare the cups themselves are followed by some simple filling suggestions; but the possibilities are endless. I recommend having some of these premade in your freezer. When surprised by drop-in guests, these can be warmed to fill with nearly anything from a well-stocked pantry and refrigerator.

They are also very sturdy, especially useful at a picnic for guests to build their own little nibbles from a selection of fillings. The Polenta Cups can be used at room temperature or filled and reheated for a warm recipe.

Casual • Picnic • Vegetarian Option

PARTY TIME PREPARATION: **Fill and/or warm and serve.**

SERVING EQUIPMENT: **A flat tray and cocktail napkins.**

BEVERAGE TO ACCOMPANY: **Beer, Gingeritas (page 195)**

Makes about 50 cups

POLENTA CUPS

6 ounces cream cheese

¼ cup freshly grated Parmesan cheese

1 cup (2 sticks) unsalted butter, cut into chunks

½ cup plus 2 tablespoons chicken or vegetable broth

¼ teaspoon salt

¼ teaspoon cayenne pepper

¼ teaspoon ground cumin

2 tablespoons minced shallots or fresh herbs

1 cup all-purpose flour

2 cups cornmeal

1. Put the cream cheese, Parmesan cheese, butter, chicken broth, spices and shallots in a food processor and pulse to combine. Add the flour and pulse to blend. Add the cornmeal and process until the dough forms a soft ball.

2. Spray the cups of a mini muffin pan with vegetable spray. Use your hands to pinch off walnut-size pieces of dough and roll into ¾-inch balls. Place each ball in a muffin cup and use your thumb to press the ball evenly into the bottom and sides of the muffin cup. They can be baked at this stage or chilled and baked up to 1 day later.

3. Preheat the oven to 350°F (180°C). Bake 22 to 25 minutes, until golden on the edges and pulling away from the muffin pan. Let cool.

Each filling recipe is enough for about 24 cups.

Grilled Shrimp and Avocado Salsa Filling

Marinate 1 pound medium, peeled and deveined shrimp in 3 tablespoons lemon juice, 2 tablespoons olive oil and 1 table-spoon minced garlic for 30 minutes. Remove the shrimp from the marinade and grill or broil until pink, about 4 minutes. Set aside.

Fill each cup with 1 teaspoon of the Avocado-Chipotle Salsa (page 144) or your favorite salsa. Top with one shrimp, halved lengthwise, and a sprig of cilantro.

Linguica and Potato Filling

Dice ¼ pound linguica sausage, andouille or Spanish chorizo. Heat 2 tablespoons olive oil in a sauté pan over medium heat. Add 1 cup finely diced new or red potatoes and sauté 3 to 5 minutes until crisply cooked and brown. Season the potatoes with salt, a pinch of red pepper flakes and ¼ teaspoon ground cumin. Add the sausage to the pan and heat through. Fill each cup with the potato mixture and top with a dollop of plain whole-milk yogurt or sour cream and a sprinkle of minced tomato and parsley.

Warm Asadero and Olive Filling

Combine ¾ cup chopped kalamata or Niçoise olives, 1½ tablespoons minced fresh rosemary and 3 tablespoons grated orange zest. Put a ¾-inch chunk of asadero cheese (Teleme or smoked mozzarella are also good in this combination) in each cup. You'll need a total of about ½ pound to fill 24 cups. Sprinkle on some of the olive mixture and put the cups on a baking sheet. Gently warm in a 350°F (180°C) oven for 5 to 6 minutes, just until the cheese slumps. Top with a generous sprinkle of cilantro.

Lemon-Basil Crostini

In my version of crostini, slices of crisp bread are brushed with intensely concentrated toppings, updating a traditional Italian snack with bright California flavors. Serve these with cheese or to accompany a salad. Or top them with a tablespoon of feta or chèvre cheese and float in green pea or lentil soup. Crushed, they're an excellent crumb topping for chicken, fish or pork. Lemon-Basil Crostini are excellent with pâté, smoked fish and egg dishes. The Red Pepper Crostini are perfect to serve with tortilla soup, to dip into guacamole or to serve with the El Paso Fondue (page 28). I serve Pesto Crostini with the Sun-Dried Tomato Spread (page 40), a cheese board and pasta.

Casual • Buffet • Picnic

PARTY TIME PREPARATIONS: None.

SERVING EQUIPMENT: Small baskets and cocktail napkins.

BEVERAGE TO ACCOMPANY: Fumé Blanc, dry sherry, vermouth with a twist of lemon

Makes 1¼ cups topping (about 60 crostini)

LEMON-BASIL TOPPING
½ cup fresh lemon juice
½ cup freshly grated Parmesan cheese
¼ cup canola oil
⅓ cup cream cheese
½ teaspoon sugar

2 teaspoons dried basil
1 clove garlic
¼ teaspoon white pepper

CROSTINI
2 (1-pound) loaves sourdough baguettes

1. **TO MAKE THE TOPPING:** Mix all the ingredients thoroughly in a food processor or blender. If making ahead, transfer to an airtight container. This mixture will keep for up to 1 month in the refrigerator.

2. Slice the baguettes very thin. Let the sliced bread dry out for a few hours before adding the topping (the dryer the bread at this stage, the crispier your finished cracker will be). Using a pastry brush, apply a generous coating of the topping on the bread. Again, air-drying for 2 hours before baking is ideal.

3. Bake at 325°F (165°C) for 15 to 18 minutes, until crispy and golden. Let the crostini cool on racks before storing. If well wrapped, they will remain crisp for up to 2 weeks.

Red Pepper Crostini Replace the lemon juice in the topping with 2 large, dried New Mexico chile pods soaked to soften in ⅓ cup boiling water and 1 tablespoon balsamic vinegar. When the pods are soft, remove the stem and seeds and puree in a food processor. Replace the dried basil with ½ teaspoon red chile flakes. Add 2 tablespoons chopped, oil-packed sun-dried tomatoes and increase the canola oil to ⅓ cup. Combine and puree as above.

Pesto Crostini Replace the topping with one recipe of Basil Pesto (page 136) or Arugula Pesto (page 138), thinned with ¼ cup heavy cream and ¼ cup of water.

TO GARNISH: THE PARSLEY CONUNDRUM

Garnishes should be more than an arbitrary addition to the landscape of a plate or an alternative to an after-dinner mint, as in the case of a parsley sprig. Like the well-chosen serving vessel, garnishes should enhance the food you have so attentively prepared. From soup to nuts, every plate can be garnished and typically benefits from some small visual element added to the basic presentation of the food. One caveat: A garnish must be edible.

I find that oversized dinner plates (11 to 13 inches) allow for the "white space" around each element of a menu that is necessary for the food to look elegant and for the garnish to matter. The use of a square or rectangular plate not only adds drama to the table, but also provides an easier shape on which to create an attractive arrangement of food. In general, make sure not to overfill a plate no matter the size or shape. To create a pretty plate, one food should not touch another; less is definitely more.

I use a garnish to accomplish one of three things:

- Introduce color or texture to a possibly blah-looking plate.

- Identify something that might be confusing. Is it a slice of creamy pâté or a slice of chocolate terrine? The thyme sprig is the tip-off.

- Contribute to the party theme. For example, if it's Halloween, the everyday chicken entrée is enlivened with carrots cut with a pumpkin-shaped cookie cutter.

Some useful, classic garnishes include: sprigs of an herb used in the recipe, edible flowers, such as nasturtium, geranium or pansy, stalks of chive or scallion, broiled mushroom caps, slices of radish or cherry tomato, herb blossoms and curls of citrus peel.

There are also many recipes like chilis, soups and stews that rely on garnishes to complete the preparation. In such recipes, garnishes are an inexorable part of the dish itself, enhancing the taste, aroma, texture and appearance of the finished dish. These preparations present a good lesson about all garnishing: Be sure to select something that complements or defines the basic recipe.

Gravlax

Salmon gravlax has been a mainstay of my party table for years. It is as elegant as lobster and as easy to prepare as a peanut butter sandwich. It delights every guest.

The tuna variation has a more robust flavor, spiced with lots of black pepper and served with pickled ginger and wasabi-spiked ponzu. Because albacore is a very delicate-fleshed fish, be sure to request the center cut, where the grain is closer, and handle it with care. To slice, put the finished albacore, well wrapped, into the freezer for about 1 hour to chill thoroughly. This will make it much easier to cut perfect, paper-thin slices.

For a large party, I like to make both and serve them in contrasting bands of color on one large platter, the peachy salmon complementing the ruby red tuna.

Formal • Buffet • Completed in Advance

PARTY TIME PREPARATIONS: Slice and arrange.

SERVING EQUIPMENT: Platter, tray, marble or wooden board and cocktail napkins.

BEVERAGE TO ACCOMPANY: Sauvignon Blanc, Pouilly-Fumé

Makes 15 to 20 servings; 1½ cups sauce

GRAVLAX
2 (1-pound) salmon fillets with skin

½ cup sugar

½ cup kosher salt

¼ cup freshly cracked white pepper

2 bunches fresh dill, chopped

DILL SAUCE
3 tablespoons cider vinegar

3½ tablespoons sugar

2 tablespoons minced fresh dill

¼ cup sour cream

½ cup plus 2 tablespoons Dijon mustard

1 tablespoon white pepper

1 tablespoon minced capers

6 tablespoons extra-virgin olive oil

TO SERVE
Thinly sliced dark bread

½ cup capers

½ cup minced scallions (white and green parts)

1. Run your fingers against the grain of the fillets to check for small pin bones. Remove any bones with tweezers. Wipe the flesh of any scales or trimmings.
2. In a flat dish large enough to hold the salmon, spread a double thickness of cheesecloth leaving a long enough border to wrap up and over the two fillets.
3. Mix the sugar, salt and pepper in a bowl.
4. Lay the first fillet, skin side down, on the cheesecloth. Sprinkle on half the sugar mixture. Using your hand, rub the mixture into the flesh. Sprinkle on the dill,

packing it down so that all of it is used to make a layer covering the fillet from edge to edge. Sprinkle the other fillet with the sugar mixture and rub it in. Place that fillet over its mate, on top of the dill layer, with skin facing up, and press into place. Wrap the cheesecloth up and over the sides and ends to create a tight package. Lay a piece of plastic wrap on top of this. Set a baking sheet flat on top of this sandwich. Put two large cans or bricks flat on the baking sheet to evenly weigh down on the salmon. Refrigerate for 4 to 5 days, turning the salmon package every 12 hours. Each time you turn, pour off the liquid that accumulates in the pan.

5.   **TO MAKE THE SAUCE:** Whisk together all the ingredients except the oil. When well combined, drizzle in the oil, while whisking. This can be made and refrigerated for up to a week in advance.

6.   **TO SERVE:** Use a clean dish towel or spatula to gently remove all of the spices and herbs from the salmon. To slice the gravlax, you will need a very sharp knife to achieve the thinnest possible slices. Start at the tail end, cutting toward the tail at a very shallow angle. Serve the slices on a platter decorated with dill fronds and accompanied by dark bread, the sauce, a bowl of capers and a bowl of minced scallions. Guests will assemble their own open-face sandwiches.

⚜ VARIATIONS

Albacore-Style Gravlax Replace the salmon with 2 pounds of very fresh center-cut albacore fillets, at least ¾ inch thick. Follow Steps 1 and 2. In Step 3, reduce the sugar and salt to 3 tablespoons each. Replace the white pepper with 3 tablespoons freshly ground black or green peppercorns and add 2 teaspoons ground ginger to the dry mix. Replace the dill with a combination of ¾ cup chopped cilantro leaves and ¾ cup chopped scallions.

In Step 4, because there is no skin on the albacore, rub the dry mix into both sides of each fillet. You may not need all of the spice mixture.

Sprinkle one side of a fillet generously with the greens mixture and place that side down on the cheesecloth. Sprinkle more greens on top, then lay on the second fillet to form a sandwich. Sprinkle the remaining greens on top. Wrap the cheesecloth up and over to form a tight packet.

Finish as above in Step 4, but refrigerate for only 36 to 48 hours, until the flesh is opaque and firm. Instead of the sauce in Step 5, prepare the Ginger-Wasabi Sauce below, or stir a little wasabi into a purchased ponzu sauce. Complete Step 6.

Serve accompanied by radish sprouts, pickled ginger and sauce. It is excellent on an endive spear or the same dark bread used for the salmon.

SELECTING FISH

Because fresh fish keeps for such a brief time, quality is of utmost importance. Given that much of this vast country has no easy access to ocean seafood, it takes more than average shopping diligence to get top-notch fish. Seek out a reputable fishmonger who takes pride in offering fish of exceptional quality. If you don't live near a specialized fish market, my best advice is to get to know the fishmonger at your supermarket. Introduce yourself, ask questions and engage him or her in conversation. These people have expertise and they want to share it with you. If you don't live near the ocean or a great fishmonger, consider sticking to your local freshwater fish or the good-quality frozen shrimp available everywhere.

Besides talking to the experts, here are a few things you can do to get the freshest fish:

- Look: For fillets or steaks, the meat should be translucent and should not appear dried out. Fresh, whole fish should still show about 80 percent of their scales (these will fall off the fish if it's been dead for a while or unrefrigerated). If you see scars or sagging skin, the fish is too old.

- Touch: Fresh whole fish should be firm. If you run your hand along the rib cage and detect that the meat has started to separate from the bones, the fish is too old.

- Smell: Fresh fish are supposed to have a briny or oceanlike smell. They do not smell "fishy."

Ginger-Wasabi Sauce

½ cup seasoned rice vinegar

2 tablespoons minced fresh ginger

2 tablespoons soy sauce

1 tablespoon fresh lime juice

½ teaspoon wasabi paste or 1 Thai chile, seeded and minced

Pinch of sugar

1 tablespoon chopped fresh cilantro, to garnish

Combine all ingredients at least 2 hours before serving, or let rest refrigerated overnight.

Stuffed Brie en Croûte

Like fondue, this is a recipe that has been around for so long it has gone through all of the stages, from new and exciting, to traditional. But it still pops up at great parties everywhere for the same solid reason: people love it. I like to serve this dish because it makes a dramatic presentation, and it can be completed up to a week in advance. I have included three simple variations that have been special favorites of my guests: wild mushroom with a layer of creamy chèvre, pecan pralines with apricot and festive cranberry with pistachio.

Formal • Buffet • Completed in Advance

PARTY TIME PREPARATION: Bake and serve.

SERVING EQUIPMENT: A large, flat pasta-style bowl that collects the runny cheese is good, or any attractive platter; 2 cheese knives or spreaders; and cocktail napkins.

BEVERAGE TO ACCOMPANY: Chardonnay, White Burgundy, Beaujolais

Makes 10 to 12 servings on a buffet

1 (2.2-pound) wheel of Brie

Filling of choice (recipes below)

1 (17-ounce) package of puff pastry, thoroughly thawed in the refrigerator

1 lightly beaten egg

1. Slice the Brie (with the skin on) in half horizontally. Lay the filling (see below), cooled if necessary, across the bottom half of the Brie and press into place. Set the top half on and again press gently to even out.
2. Roll both sheets of pastry out to about 12-inch squares on a lightly floured board. Trim to 12-inch circles.
3. Place the filled wheel of Brie on one sheet of pastry and pull the pastry up and over the sides; it will lap over about an inch. Brush the edge of the pastry with cold water and pleat the excess to lay flat on the cheese.
4. Lay the second sheet on the countertop and invert the half-covered Brie onto this pleated side down. Fold the bottom sheet up and over, to overlap the first sheet. Brush cold water on this edge and press into the first pastry layer to seal.
5. Refrigerate for at least 2 hours before baking or freeze well wrapped for up to 2 weeks. If frozen, let defrost at room temperature for 1 hour before baking.
6. **TO BAKE:** Preheat the oven to 400°F (205°C). Brush the top of the Brie with lightly beaten egg. Place on a parchment paper–lined baking sheet. Bake 35 to 40 minutes,

until the pastry is golden. Let rest 5 to 10 minutes (or up to 20 minutes if you need the time) before serving with wedges of bread, crackers and fruit.

🔅 VARIATIONS

Chèvre and Mushroom Filling

2 tablespoons unsalted butter	Kosher salt and freshly ground coarse black pepper
½ pound button or wild mushrooms, sliced thinly	9 ounces chèvre, broken into chunks
2 teaspoons minced fresh thyme	Freshly grated nutmeg
2 tablespoons dry vermouth or apple brandy	

1. Melt the butter in a sauté pan over medium heat. When bubbling, add the mushrooms and thyme; sauté until soft and golden. Add the vermouth and simmer 1 to 2 minutes. Season lightly with salt and pepper. Set aside to cool.

2. **TO ASSEMBLE:** Layer the mushroom mixture over the bottom half of the Brie; top with the chèvre. Sprinkle lightly with the nutmeg. Cover with the top half of the Brie. Complete as above.

Pecan Praline and Apricot Filling

3 tablespoons unsalted butter	¾ cup chopped, dried California apricots
1 cup pecan halves	½ cup packed light brown sugar
6 tablespoons granulated sugar	1 or 2 tablespoons of minced fresh thyme or lavender (optional)
Pinch kosher salt	

Melt the butter in a large sauté pan. Add pecan halves and sauté 3 to 4 minutes, until toasted. Add the granulated sugar and salt and continue to sauté until the sugar melts and coats the nuts, 4 to 5 minutes. Pour onto a greased baking sheet pan to cool. Roughly chop the pecans.

Layer the chopped pecans over the bottom half of the Brie with the chopped apricots and brown sugar. Sprinkle with the thyme for a sophisticated touch. Complete as above.

Dried Cranberry and Pistachio Filling

¾ cup dried cranberries or cherries

¾ cup chopped, toasted pistachios

½ cup packed light brown sugar

3 tablespoons kirsch or cognac

Sprinkle the cranberries, pistachios and brown sugar over the bottom half of the Brie. Drizzle with the kirsch. Complete as above.

Chicken Liver Porcini Pâté

Everyone enjoys the luxury of pâté, but often the idea of making it seems like an overwhelming project. This simple recipe proves that making your own is a breeze, and well worth the effort. The rich, silky texture is clearly homemade, and the special garnishes make it beautiful on a buffet or cocktail table. The smoked trout variation is a wonderfully sophisticated option to the ubiquitous smoked salmon spreads.

Formal • Buffet • Completed in Advance

PARTY TIME PREPARATIONS: Unmold, garnish and add bread or crackers and fruit.

SERVING EQUIPMENT: A medium platter or cutting board, 1 or 2 spreader knives, basket for bread or crackers, and cocktail napkins.

BEVERAGE TO ACCOMPANY: Dry sherry, dry vermouth with a twist of lemon, medium-bodied Zinfandel

Makes 8 to 10 servings

PÂTÉ
3 tablespoons snipped chives plus several whole spears

1½ ounces dried porcini mushrooms

¼ cup Madeira

1 pound chicken livers, trimmed

1 cup chicken broth

Freshly ground coarse black pepper

1 medium onion, chopped (about 1 cup)

½ cup (1 stick) plus 6 tablespoons unsalted butter, cut into chunks

2 cloves garlic, peeled

1 teaspoon freshly grated nutmeg

1½ teaspoons salt

1 teaspoon finely ground dried thyme

¼ teaspoon white pepper

¼ cup brandy

½ cup roughly chopped dried prunes

½ cup toasted pine nuts or walnuts

TO SERVE
Sliced green apples

Crackers or crostini

1. Line a 3- to 4-cup terrine or mold with plastic wrap. Spray with cooking spray. Arrange some of the whole chives (or other fresh herb) in the bottom of the mold. This creates a decoration on the top of the pâté when it's unmolded.

2. Put the dried porcini and Madeira into a small microwave-safe container; add up to 1 tablespoon water if necessary to cover. Cover lightly with plastic wrap and heat for 60 seconds on High. Set aside and let cool to room temperature.

3. Clean the chicken livers well, cutting off any fat or tendons. In a medium saucepan, bring the broth, pepper and 2 cups of water to a boil. Add the livers and onion and reduce the heat. Simmer for 10 to 12 minutes, until cooked through. Drain livers and onion. Let cool and transfer to the bowl of a food processor.

4. Add all the remaining ingredients except the prunes and pine nuts. Process in pulses until smooth. Fold in the prunes.

5. Transfer the mixture to the lined mold. Tap the mold gently on the countertop to settle out any bubbles. Then smooth the top, cover tightly and refrigerate for at least 4 hours or up to 4 days before unmolding to serve.

6. **TO SERVE:** Loosen the plastic wrap, invert the mold over a serving plate and slide out. Press the chopped nuts gently into the sides of the pâté and serve with apples and crackers.

✺ VARIATION

Smoked Trout Pâté Skip Steps 2 and 3 entirely since the trout is already cooked. In Step 4, use a ¾-pound smoked trout, with all of the fine bones removed, in place of the chicken livers. Replace the nutmeg with 2 tablespoons of well-drained bottled horseradish and, because the fish is quite salty, eliminate the salt. Do not use the prunes. To enhance the delicate flavor of the trout, add 1½ tablespoons minced fresh dill, 1½ tablespoons finely grated lemon zest, 1 tablespoon lemon juice and ¼ cup minced scallions. Instead of Madeira, use vodka or Aquavit.

When the pâté is unmolded, instead of pine nuts, you could press about ½ cup minced chives or dill around the sides.

Classic Swiss Fondue

Fondue is such a traditional recipe that in some eras it has been considered unsophisticated. Au contraire. Fondue is great party food; it is interactive, fun and based on one of the most popular ingredients on any buffet, cheese. The simple recipes that follow give you the platform for many experiments on your own. The Italian Fontina Fondue is very elegant with fennel and cured salami for dipping, and the El Paso Fondue can also be used as the topping for a delicious nacho platter.

Another great optional use for any of these fondues is as the cheese component for a gourmet mac and cheese casserole; toss cooked pasta with the fondue, top with additional cheese or bread crumbs and bake at 350°F (180°C) until bubbling.

Casual • Vegetarian Option • Kid Appeal

PARTY TIME PREPARATIONS: Heat and mix.

SERVING EQUIPMENT: Fondue pot (or small chafer), fondue forks or skewers, small plates and cocktail napkins.

BEVERAGE TO ACCOMPANY: Viognier, Pinot Grigio, Alsatian Pinot Gris

Serves 8 to 10 as an appetizer or 4 as an entrée; makes 3 cups

FONDUE

2 teaspoons cornstarch

3 tablespoons kirsch

1 clove garlic, smashed

1 to 1¼ cups dry white wine

1 tablespoon fresh lemon juice

1 pound Gruyère or 8 ounces Gruyère and 8 ounces Emmentaler, grated (4 cups)

⅛ teaspoon freshly grated nutmeg

White pepper

TO SERVE

Bread cubes, crostini or pita wedges, green apple wedges, blanched carrots or cauliflower

1. In a small bowl, whisk the cornstarch into the kirsch to dissolve.
2. Rub the garlic clove around the inside of a heavy saucepan over medium heat and then drop it in. Add the 1 cup white wine and lemon juice and bring to a gentle simmer. Add the shredded cheese, one handful at a time, stirring constantly with a wooden spoon.
3. When the cheese is completely melted into the liquid, add the kirsch mixture and whisk to blend. Let simmer several minutes to thicken. If the mixture is too thick, stir in some additional wine. Season with the nutmeg and white pepper. Transfer immediately to a fondue pot and serve with bread cubes, fruit or vegetables.

Italian Fontina Fondue In Step 1, replace the kirsch with 3 tablespoons Marsala and whisk in the cornstarch.

In Step 2, increase the garlic to 2 cloves and replace the white wine with dry vermouth. Replace the Gruyère cheese with a combination of 1½ cups grated Gruyère and 2 cups grated Fontina. Proceed with Step 2 as above.

In Step 3, when smooth and creamy, sprinkle in 1 cup freshly shredded Parmesan cheese and blend well until it melts. Add the Marsala mixture. Finish with a pinch of red chile flakes instead of the nutmeg.

Transfer to a warmed fondue serving pot and serve immediately with focaccia or breadsticks, artichoke hearts, red and yellow pepper wedges, slices of fennel and slices of hard salami.

El Paso Fondue In Step 1, dissolve the cornstarch in 5 tablespoons of half-and-half.

In Step 2, increase the garlic to 2 cloves and add 2 teaspoons cumin seeds. Replace the wine and lemon juice with 1 cup dark beer and use a combination of 2½ cups grated Monterey Jack and 2 cups grated sharp Cheddar instead of the Gruyère. In Step 3, add the half-and-half mixture and whisk to blend. After simmering to thicken, add ½ teaspoon cayenne pepper and ⅓ cup chopped cilantro instead of the nutmeg and white pepper.

Transfer to a warmed fondue serving pot and serve immediately with cherry tomatoes, tortilla chips, wedges of spicy cooked sausage and jicama wedges.

NOTE: You don't have to buy a specific "fondue vessel." A small chafing dish, which is a great all-round entertaining purchase, works just as well. Fondue is easiest heated on the stove and transferred to a fondue pot or chafing dish to serve. Fill the pot less than half full; if it's too full it's easier to lose your dunking medium and harder to keep well mixed.

THE CHEESE COURSE

A cheese course is easy to prepare and one of the most universally popular treats, no matter where it appears in the progress of the meal. Cheese courses can be served as an appetizer, after the entrée or as a dessert. In Italy cheese is often served as an hors d'oeuvre to stimulate the appetite and is served alongside cured meats like prosciutto, roasted peppers and cured olives. In England cheeses may be served after the entrée as a transitional course with a glass of port to effectively slow down the dinner and encourage conversation. In France the cheese course is often served after the dessert to extend the pleasure of the meal. These cheese trays often include fresh fruits and berries as well as dried fruits and fruit pastes. Late-harvest wines and sauternes are often served.

Today a great selection of cheeses, fulfilling all the basic requirements for variety of taste, texture and intensity, can be assembled from the cheese case of most well-stocked supermarkets. A specialty cheese shop will obviously provide more unusual or exotic examples within each category, however you can easily use the combinations below to put together sophisticated pairings from your local grocery. When you have mastered the nuances of which flavors, textures, aromas and shapes you prefer, you may want to seek out a specialty cheese shop to expand your palate.

When planning a cheese course, allow for 1 to 1½ ounces of cheese per guest. A cheese board should consist of a selection of at least three and up to seven or eight cheeses with varying textures, flavors and colors. When planning, also keep in mind the balance of soft and mild to hard and sharp. Paired with simple accompaniments, this cheese sampler offers the host an opportunity for easy creativity. Aged cheese should be removed from the refrigerator an hour ahead of time. Fresh cheeses should be kept cold until serving.

The presentation can be either rustic or formal. Cheeses may be served on granite or marble platters, wooden or wicker trays or other interesting flat surfaces. The accompaniments are often arranged in between the different types of cheeses. I usually decorate my cheese tray with fresh herbs or French paper leaves, fig or lemon leaves and edible flowers. A separate knife or spreader should be provided for each cheese. Serve with warm, crusty bread or crackers and wine. If the cheese course includes an assortment of cheeses with strong flavors, several types of wine might be offered.

Below are some examples of cheese and wine pairings.

CHEESE AND WINE AS AN APPETIZER

CHEESE: Mozzarella di bufala, Fontina (semisoft cheese), Gorgonzola (a blue-veined cheese), Parmigiano-Reggiano

ACCOMPANIMENTS: Hard salami, assorted olives and roasted red peppers

WINE: Chianti

CHEESE: Teleme, Asiago, Maytag Blue, Vermont Cheddar

ACCOMPANIMENTS: Crackers, sliced pears and toasted walnuts

WINE: Pinot Noir

CHEESE: Cotija, Manchego, Cabrales

ACCOMPANIMENTS: Sliced Spanish chorizo or serrano ham and olives

WINE: Rioja

CHEESE AND WINE AS A TRANSITIONAL COURSE

CHEESE: Brie, Stilton, Cheshire (sharp English Cheddar)

ACCOMPANIMENTS: Roasted almonds

WINE: Port

CHEESE: Camembert, Gouda, Montbriac, Vella Dry Jack

ACCOMPANIMENTS: French oil-cured olives, roasted walnuts and pecans

WINE: Dry sherry

CHEESE AND WINE AS A DESSERT

CHEESE: Montrachet (mild goat cheese), Bel Paese, Roquefort, Gruyère

ACCOMPANIMENTS: Figs, quince paste and toasted hazelnuts

WINE: Late-harvest Riesling or Sauterne

CHEESE: Brillat-Savarin, Fontina, Comte, Raclette

ACCOMPANIMENTS: Peaches, pears and raspberries

WINE: Sancerre or Champagne

Tarte Pissaladiere

The Provençal kitchen is noted for olives, seafood, lavender, honey, rosemary, lemon and olive oil. This simply luscious tart, a popular street food in southern France, combines many of those tastes. The quick, crisp crust can be replaced with purchased puff pastry for a less rustic look. I like it both ways.

Served in bite-size wedges, either warm from the oven or at room temperature, it is a boldly flavored hors d'oeuvre. Served with a green salad and red wine, this is a sophisticated main course for a luncheon or light supper. For either purpose, the earthy-hued slices look lovely garnished with a sprig of fresh herb. For anchovy phobes, the salty flavor can be contributed by crumbled feta cheese.

Buffet • Picnic • Vegetarian Option

PARTY TIME PREPARATIONS: Garnish and serve.

SERVING EQUIPMENT: Flat platter or tray; to keep warm, if desired, a hot tray; tongs or pie server; and cocktail napkins.

BEVERAGE TO ACCOMPANY: Fumé Blanc, dry Gewürztraminer

Makes 20 to 24 hors d'oeuvres or 8 to 10 entrée servings

CRUST

1¼ cups all-purpose flour

½ teaspoon kosher salt

¼ cup unsalted cold butter, cut into pieces

2 tablespoons olive oil

3 to 4 tablespoons cold water

FILLING

3 tablespoons olive oil

2½ pounds sweet onions, (such as Maui or Vidalia) or yellow onions, thinly sliced (about 8 cups)

3 to 4 cloves garlic, minced

2 bay leaves

1½ teaspoons chopped fresh thyme or rosemary

1 tablespoon capers, drained

Kosher salt and freshly ground coarse black pepper, to taste

1 (2-ounce) can anchovy fillets in olive oil, drained

15 to 20 pitted Niçoise or kalamata olives

1. **TO MAKE THE CRUST:** Combine all the ingredients, except the water, in a food processor. Using pulses, briefly process until the mixture resembles coarse meal. Continuing to pulse, add enough water so that dough forms moist clumps. Gather dough into a ball. Flatten dough into a disc, wrap and refrigerate for at least 2 hours or up to 2 days.

2. **TO MAKE THE FILLING:** Heat the olive oil in a heavy 10- to 14-inch skillet over medium-low heat. Add the onions, garlic, bay leaves and thyme. Stir to mix. Cover well and cook, stirring occasionally, until onions are very tender, about 45 minutes. Uncover and continue to cook until most of the liquid evaporates and the onions are golden (not brown), about 20 minutes. The onions will be the texture of rough-cut marmalade. Stir in the capers, remove the bay leaves and season with salt and pepper. Cover and refrigerate for up to 2 days.

3. Preheat the oven to 425°F (220°C). Lightly oil a baking sheet. If chilled overnight, allow the crust and filling to warm slightly at room temperature. Roll out the dough on a floured surface to a 10- to 12-inch circle or square. Transfer the dough to the prepared baking sheet. Crimp up the edge of the pastry all around to form a lip on the crust. Spread the onion mixture evenly across the dough. Arrange the anchovies and olives in a decorative pattern across the onions. I make Xs with the anchovies to create a diamond pattern with olives dotted in the openings.

4. Bake the tarte until crisp and the edges are golden, about 30 minutes. Allow to cool for a few minutes before slicing to serve. A serrated knife or pizza cutter works best for slicing.

❦ VARIATION

Anchovy-Less Tarte Pissaladiere Replace the anchovies in Step 3 with ½ cup crumbled feta cheese.

SEAFOOD BAR

There are three species of creatures who when they seem coming are going, when they seem going they come: diplomats, women, and crabs.

—John Hay, 19th century American diplomat

Fresh seafood occupies a romantic spot in the heart of most everyone. Like champagne, it signifies a special, luxurious occasion. This is the kind of feeling I like to evoke for my guests with a seafood bar. As an additional inducement to the host, this buffet requires virtually no preparation, just a little time to create a beautiful setting.

Build your seafood bar in a giant platter, copper wine tub, flat basket lined with plastic and greens, terra-cotta saucers, plastic-lined wheelbarrow or kitchen sink. One of my favorite seafood bars for a crowd was assembled in a tiny dinghy that we angled across a garden wall.

No more than half an hour before the guests are to arrive, fill the bar with crushed ice draped with fresh seaweed or clusters of fresh green herbs and seashells. Let the seaweed trail off the ice and onto the table. Arrange the shellfish on the half shell and crab claws and shrimp directly on the decorated ice. Any prepared dishes can be put in small shells or dishes and settled into the ice. There should be at least two prepared sauces, one spicy and one mild, and lots of lemon wedges both on the ice and in bowls on the side.

If you plan to leave the display out for more than 30 minutes, plan to drain off the water that will collect in the platter from the rapidly melting ice (see note, page 34). Make sure to have one or two bowls on the table for discarded shrimp tails and empty shells.

A hollowed artichoke, large scallop shells and children's beach pails and plastic shovels are all good containers to tuck into the ice to hold the sauces for dipping. Clear containers also look good as they reflect the sparkle of the ice.

While a seafood platter is a wonderfully easy, impressive hors d'oeuvre solution for eight, it will look truly spectacular as a bounteous focal point at a gathering of forty or fifty. For a group that size, you will want to have someone there shucking oysters and replenishing the seafood in response to the inevitable enthusiasm of the guests.

A simple seafood platter to serve 12 guests might contain:

- 14 oysters or clams on the half-shell
- 18 large (16 to 20 per pound) boiled shrimp with the tail on
- 14 snow crab claws
- Rouille (page 140) and Horseradish-Dijon Butter (page 74)
- Lemon wedges

For a larger crowd, or for a more extended buffet period, the bar could be expanded to include:

- Smoked fish or Gravlax (page 19) with a mustard sauce
- Caviar
- Cracked King crab legs
- Cooked mussels in the shell

To prepare boiled shrimp: Bring 2 quarts of water, a pinch of salt, a sprig of parsley or other fresh herb and one sliced lemon to a rolling boil. Add 1 pound large shrimp and cook, uncovered, until bright pink, 3 to 4 minutes. Drain and peel, leaving the tail on. Chill for up to 24 hours.

To prepare steamed clams and mussels: It is essential to start with fresh, lively shellfish. If any of the clams or mussel shells are open, tap them lightly on the countertop. If the shell doesn't close, discard it.

Scrub the clams well and put in a bowl with lots of cold salted water (about ⅓ cup of salt to 1 gallon of water) to cover. Let stand for about 20 minutes to draw out the sand they often contain. Rinse well. Mussels should be scrubbed and their fibrous "beards" pulled off just before cooking.

Mussels and clams can be steamed in the same fashion to be served on a seafood bar. Place 18 green-lipped mussels or 2 dozen littleneck clams in a large saucepan. Add ½ cup white wine or water, a pinch of salt and some fresh herbs. Cover and place over high heat. Let steam until all shells are opened, about 5 minutes. Remove with a slotted spoon. Wrap and refrigerate for up to 24 hours. Serve on the shell, with small cocktail forks or wooden picks handy, to pluck them from their shells. To create a lovely warm appetizer, add tomatoes, chiles or herbs to the cooking broth.

To prepare raw shellfish: Raw oysters and clams should be shucked at the last minute, no longer than an hour before serving. Replace the top shell after opening and hold the reconstructed mollusks in the refrigerator covered with a damp towel. Try to save the liquor that rests in the bottom shell; this contains the concentrated briny taste of the ocean that is the elegant essence of fresh oysters and clams.

NOTE: A professional seafood pan has a hole drilled in the bottom with a plastic hose attached, which drips into a bucket hidden somewhere from sight. You could re-create the same practical setup on a smaller scale by wedging a cake cooling rack into a bowl of a size that suspends the rack 2 to 3 inches above the bottom of the bowl. Pile the ice on the rack with the seafood on top. The openings in the rack will allow the water from the melting ice to accumulate in the bottom of the bowl without turning the entire container into a soupy mess.

Hot Scampi Dip

Hot dips fulfil a very useful role in your menu. Easily prepared ahead of time, the dips' rich, warm gooeyness make an elegant appeal to everyone's lust for comfort food with panache. I often serve the Mushroom and Artichoke Heart Dip over noodles (before the final baking in Step 7) as a vegetarian entrée on a cold winter's night.

Formal • Buffet • Vegetarian Options

PARTY TIME PREPARATIONS: Heat and serve.

SERVING EQUIPMENT: The dish it was baked in placed on a lining platter with 2 knives, basket for bread or crackers and cocktail napkins.

BEVERAGE TO ACCOMPANY: Fumé Blanc, dry sherry, vermouth with a twist of lemon

Makes about 4 cups

1 pound deveined, peeled raw shrimp	4 ounces Fontina or white Cheddar, grated
4 tablespoons unsalted butter	½ cup freshly grated Parmesan cheese
⅓ cup minced shallots	1 teaspoon red chile flakes
3 tablespoons minced garlic	2 teaspoons dried oregano or thyme
3 tablespoons dry white wine	¼ cup fresh lemon or lime juice
¼ cup chopped fresh basil	¼ teaspoon kosher salt
½ cup chopped green onions (white and green parts)	Freshly ground coarse black pepper, to taste
⅔ cup half-and-half	2 slices sourdough bread, cubed
8 ounces cream cheese	

1. Chop the shrimp.
2. Heat 3 tablespoons of the butter in a sauté pan to bubbling. Add the shallots and sauté to soften, about 3 minutes. Add the garlic and sauté 2 minutes. Add the shrimp and sauté, stirring, until pink and firm, about 4 minutes. Add the white wine and simmer for 2 to 3 minutes to loosen all of the pan juices. Set aside.
3. Combine the basil and green onions in a bowl.
4. Heat the half-and-half in a saucepan over medium heat until hot, but not boiling. Whisk in the cream cheese in chunks until well blended. Add the Fontina cheese and ¼ cup of the Parmesan cheese by handfuls, whisking until thoroughly melted. Add the chile flakes, oregano, half of the green onion mixture and all of the cooked shrimp mixture. Whisk to blend and simmer gently for 2 to 3 minutes. Remove

from heat and whisk in the lemon juice, salt and pepper. Transfer the mixture to a ½-quart baking/serving dish. The dish can be completed through this stage and refrigerated for up to 24 hours.

5. Preheat the oven to 400°F (205°C). Sprinkle the top with sourdough cubes, then the remaining Parmesan cheese and drizzle with remaining 1 tablespoon of butter. Bake for 18 to 20 minutes, until browned and bubbling. Serve sprinkled with remaining green onion mixture.

🎋 VARIATION

Mushroom and Artichoke Heart Dip Cover 1 ounce dried porcini mushrooms in ½ cup boiling water until softened, about 30 minutes. Drain and reserve the liquid. Chop the mushrooms.

In Step 1, replace the shrimp with 3 cups chopped fresh shiitake or white button mushrooms plus the chopped porcini and sauté as directed in Step 2 until the mushrooms are soft and golden, about 8 minutes. Add the reserved porcini liquor, along with the wine and 1 cup drained artichoke hearts, sliced in quarters. In Step 3, thyme would be the more complementary dried herb. Proceed with original recipe instructions.

PRIMER ON CAVIARS AND ROES

Caviar is to dining what a sable coat is to a girl in an evening dress.
—Ludwig Bemelmans

Like other extravagances, caviar can be (but is not always) expensive and, in the case of some snooty retailers, exclusive. Don't let money or attitude stop you from bringing this quintessential celebration food into your special feasts. Because fresh caviar may only be available at your local grocer during the holidays, plan to include it as part of your holiday entertaining. The rest of the year you will only find pasteurized caviar. This is not a stand-alone delicacy and shouldn't be served as a center of the tray hors d'oeuvre. I sometimes use the pasteurised product as a garnish to devilled eggs or individual canapés.

CLASSIC CAVIAR SERVICE

Nestle the tin or jar of caviar in a shallow bowl, full of crushed ice. Serve the caviar with nonreactive spoons or those made of natural material, such as bone, horn, crystal or mother-of-pearl (sterling silver will give the caviar a metallic taste and discolor the beads). Have a different spoon for each species of caviar so delicate and unique flavors are not confused.

Traditionally, caviar is offered with either blini (dollar-sized buckwheat pancakes), toast points or simple, boiled red potatoes. Accompaniments include chopped egg white; chopped egg yolk; chopped shallot, onion or chives; and crème fraîche. Serve with chilled vodka, dry champagne or sparkling wine.

Only sturgeon roe from the Caspian Sea can legally be called caviar. In the United States, retailers must list the species—salmon, whitefish, paddlefish, sturgeon—before the word *caviar*. Some fine domestic "caviars" include:

- Yellowstone River Paddlefish Caviar: A great value with notes of melon. It's ideal with traditional caviar service.

- Domestic White Sturgeon: An aquaculture product with a mild, nutty flavor.

Some imported classics (from least to most expensive) include Sevruga, Osetra and Beluga.

Provençal Olive and Citrus Spread or Dip

The longer you cook, the more clearly you see how interrelated recipes are. In my experience, the flavors that make an excellent spread are also great in dips; you can use the following recipes for both. The root recipes are for the spread consistency and based on cream cheese. To turn any of them into a dip, simply delete the butter in the recipe or add yogurt or sour cream to thin the texture of the finished dip.

Casual • Buffet • Vegetarian Option

PARTY TIME PREPARATIONS: Garnish and serve.

SERVING EQUIPMENT: Attractive 3-cup bowl or ramekin, 2 spreading knives, basket for bread or crackers and cocktail napkins.

BEVERAGE TO ACCOMPANY: Fumé Blanc, dry sherry, vermouth with a twist of lemon

Makes about 2½ cups

BASE	FLAVORING
10 ounces chèvre	½ cup chopped, pitted kalamata or Niçoise olives
8 ounces cream cheese	2 tablespoons brandy
4 tablespoons unsalted butter	2 teaspoons minced rosemary
⅛ teaspoon freshly grated nutmeg	3 cloves garlic
1 tablespoon minced garlic	4 tablespoons unsalted butter
1 tablespoon minced shallot	1 tablespoon grated lemon zest
¼ teaspoon kosher salt	2 tablespoons grated orange zest
¼ teaspoon white pepper	3 tablespoons orange juice

1. Blend all of the cheese base ingredients in a food processor using pulses. Add the flavor ingredients and pulse to mix completely without overwhipping.

2. Refrigerate for at least 2 hours or up to 5 days. Serve garnished with chopped chives or lavender blossoms.

Roasted Eggplant Spread For the flavoring: Cook 2 whole large eggplant (about 1¼ pounds each) by first pricking and then roasting on a baking sheet at 400°F (205°C) for about 50 minutes, until charred appearing and extremely soft. Split open, scoop out the pulp and mince.

For the flavoring in Step 1, substitute the roasted eggplant, plus 3 tablespoons minced parsley, ¼ teaspoon ground coriander, ¼ teaspoon ground cinnamon and ¼ cup fresh lemon juice. Pulse very gently just to mix, not puree. Taste for salt and pepper. Proceed as above. Serve garnished with toasted pine nuts.

Coconut-Crab Dip For the flavoring in Step 1, substitute 1½ cups lump crabmeat, 3 tablespoons coconut milk, 1 teaspoon minced fresh ginger, 2 tablespoons dry sherry, 1 tablespoon chutney, 3 tablespoons minced cilantro and a dash of hot pepper sauce. Proceed as above. Garnish with roasted peanuts or toasted coconut.

Roasted Mushroom Dip Heat a large sauté pan over medium heat. Add two tablespoons unsalted butter. When the butter is sizzling, add 2 cups chopped portobello or shiitake mushrooms and 2 tablespoons minced garlic. Sauté until all of the moisture has evaporated. Add 3 tablespoons dry vermouth to the pan and let it simmer until the mushrooms have absorbed most of the vermouth. Set aside to cool.

Substitute the mushroom mixture for the flavoring in Step 1. Add 1 tablespoon grated lemon zest and 1 tablespoon minced fresh thyme. Proceed as above. Serve garnished with thyme sprigs and slivers of radish.

Mediterranean Sesame-Oregano Spread or Dip

Of the many styles of spreads, some of the most versatile are those in which a bean puree forms the base. I have included recipes for spreads based on cannellini and garbanzo purees. In addition to being served in a tub to spread on great bread or thinned out to dip vegetables or chips into, all of these spreads can be used as the basic filling for the endlessly useful "roll-up sandwich" (see Party Pinwheels, page 42). Flexibility is the byword in an entertaining kitchen.

Casual • Buffet • Vegetarian Option

PARTY TIME PREPARATIONS: Garnish and serve.

SERVING EQUIPMENT: Attractive 3-cup bowl or ramekin, 2 spreading knives, basket for bread or crackers and cocktail napkins.

BEVERAGE TO ACCOMPANY: Beer, Peach Sangria (page 193), Pinot Noir

Makes about 3½ cups

BASE	FLAVORING
1 (15-ounce) can garbanzo beans, drained	½ cup tahini
1 (15-ounce) can cannellini beans, drained	3 tablespoons fresh lemon juice
1 tablespoon minced garlic	½ teaspoon ground cumin
2 tablespoons fresh lemon juice	¼ teaspoon cayenne pepper
¼ cup extra-virgin olive oil	3 tablespoons chopped fresh oregano
½ teaspoon kosher salt	3 tablespoons chopped fresh mint
¼ teaspoon freshly ground coarse black pepper	Roasted pistachios, to garnish

1. Puree the base ingredients in a food processor.
2. Add the flavor ingredients and pulse to blend thoroughly. Taste for salt and pepper. Refrigerate at least 2 hours or up to 5 days. Serve garnished with pistachios.

❧ VARIATION

Sun-Dried Tomato Spread Follow the directions in Step 1. For the flavor component, substitute ¼ cup chopped fresh basil, 2 tablespoons chopped fresh oregano or

DIPPERS AND SCOOPERS

One of the challenges of a stand-up cocktail or hors d'oeuvre party is snacking logistics. As a guest, how many times have you had to balance a plate on your head in order to shake someone's hand without spilling your wine? Undoubtedly the answer is, "Too many." Spare your guests the cocktail-hour contortions and plan a menu around foods that can benefit from skewers or edible vessels as simple as a spear of endive or puff pastry tartlet. Your guests will thank you and you'll have fewer dishes to do. Just be sure to have plenty of napkins at the ready for foodie fingers.

mint, and 1 teaspoon minced garlic for the ingredients above. When well mixed, stir in ⅔ cup chopped, oil-packed sun-dried tomatoes (including some of their oil). Serve garnished with basil leaves.

PARTY PINWHEELS

The pinwheel is the inventive use of soft lavosh or large flour tortillas, usually 14 to 18 inches in diameter, to create an attractive spiraled sandwich. I serve them in ½-inch slices as a hearty hors d'oeuvre for a casual party or in 3- to 4-inch wedges as a main course at a picnic.

TIPS ON MAKING A PINWHEEL

Begin by laying the lavosh or tortilla out on a sheet of foil or plastic wrap that extends beyond the bread by about 2 inches. Spread ¾ cup of any of the spreads listed below, or your favorite spread, across the wrap, leaving empty a 2-inch border at one end. Layer the suggested toppings across the spread in about the same quantity as you would use to generously top a pizza. Anything crunchy or curly, like lettuce or sprouts, should be added last. Curl over the filled end to form a tight cylinder and use the plastic to help finish rolling toward the uncoated end. Tuck the plastic wrap securely around the completed log and refrigerate for at least 4 hours or overnight. As it chills the sandwich will mold itself into the log shape.

To serve, slice diagonally across the log to create a pretty spiral pattern.

Some pinwheel combinations that my guests have enjoyed include:

- Chèvre, bacon and tomato with shredded romaine lettuce.
- Roasted Mushroom Dip (page 39), grated kasseri cheese, sliced, roasted peppers, sliced tomato and arugula.
- Sun-Dried Tomato Spread (page 40), grilled onions, thinly sliced roast turkey and chopped radishes.
- Roasted Eggplant Spread (page 39), poached, shredded chicken, sliced grapes and julienned cucumber.
- Mediterranean Sesame-Oregano Spread (page 40), crumbled feta, sliced, grilled eggplant, sliced tomato and watercress.
- Cream cheese, chopped pistachios, smoked salmon, chopped watercress and dill.

Party Nuts

Flavorful, homemade, spiced nuts are a classic for every reception menu. I usually make both the candied and spiced nuts to combine for an exciting flavor contrast. When I am serving both recipes, I prepare each utilizing a different nut. I also use the candied nuts to sprinkle on mashed yams, pumpkin polenta or a salad of bitter greens and blue cheese. They stay crisp for up to 1 week if sealed in an airtight container with a piece of parchment or waxed paper in the bottom.

Formal Occasion • Buffet • Completed in Advance

PARTY TIME PREPARATIONS: None.

SERVING EQUIPMENT: Small bowls and cocktail napkins.

BEVERAGE TO ACCOMPANY: Fumé Blanc, dry sherry, vermouth with a twist of lemon

Makes about 2 cups

Candied Nuts

1 tablespoon canola oil	3 tablespoons sugar
1 tablespoon unsalted butter	2 tablespoons maple syrup
2½ teaspoons five spice powder	2 cups walnuts, pecans or blanched almonds (or mixed), toasted (see note, page 45)
¼ teaspoon white pepper	
1½ teaspoons kosher or sea salt	

1. Line a baking sheet with foil and spray lightly with vegetable spray.
2. Heat the oil and butter in 10-inch sauté pan over medium heat. Add spices and salt and sauté until fragrant, about 30 seconds. Stir in sugar and maple syrup and let melt. Add the nuts and stir with a wooden spoon until the sugar mixture is amber and bubbly and the nuts are thoroughly coated, 4 to 5 minutes.
3. Transfer the nuts to the oiled foil. Working quickly, spread the nuts in a single layer, trying to separate the nuts from each other. Let cool.

❆ VARIATION

Replace the five spice powder in Step 2 with ½ teaspoon ground cardamom, ½ teaspoon ground ginger, 1 teaspoon curry powder and ½ teaspoon ground cinnamon. Proceed as above.

Makes about 2½ cups

THE OLIVE SAMPLER

The olive tree is certainly the richest gift of heaven.
—Thomas Jefferson

There are a remarkable variety of olives available these days, most of them imported. Many upscale stores even have "olive bars" where you can help yourself from a selection of 30 or more varieties. This is a boon to the crafty, casual host. Keep some of these olive varieties in your refrigerator along with some excellent cheeses (see box, page 29) and you've got cocktail nibbles in a minute. The list below describes the most available types:

- Picholine, France: Green; in a lemon brine; small, meaty olives; "serve 'ems and eat 'ems" with Lillet or dry French rosé in summer.

- Lucques, Italy: Bright green; in a lemon brine; clear, crunchy flesh, with subtle flavor and notes of fresh almonds and avocados; just eat them or use in Chicken Provençal (page 99).

- Oil-Cured, Morocco: Dark black, wrinkled; pruney texture with mellow flavor and only slightly bitter finish; ideal on Grilled Pizza (page 114) with tangy tomato sauce and fresh herbs.

- Oil-Cured, Provence: Dark black, wrinkled; pruney texture with all the joy of the Moroccan and added bonus of herbes de Provence. Excellent on the Tarte Pissaladiere (page 31).

Spiced Nuts

1 egg white	½ teaspoon ground ginger
2½ cups unsalted almonds, cashews or peanuts, roasted (see note, page 45)	½ teaspoon cayenne pepper
3 teaspoons ground cumin	2 teaspoons sugar
1 teaspoon chili powder	2 teaspoons kosher salt

1. Preheat the oven to 300°F (150°C). Line a baking sheet with foil and spray with vegetable oil.

2. Whip the egg white with a few drops of water until frothy. Add the nuts to the egg white and toss to mix. Use a slotted spoon or strainer to transfer the nuts to a sec-

- **Sicilian-style, California:** Green (pitted/with pit); brine cured; large, classic taste; ideal cocktail olive of Martinis (page 197).

- **Catalan, Spain:** Green; large; in magnificent brine of fruit, peppers and spices; with a cured meat finish, like salami or coppa; a favorite of forlorn vegetarians. Great addition to a vegetarian brochette.

- **Calabrese, Italy:** Green; medium; spiced, garlic brine.

- **Gaeta, Italy:** Black/burgundy; small, round; brine cured with slightly bitter taste; perfect for Crostini (page 16).

- **Kalamata, Greece:** Black/purple (pitted/with pit); mild, bright flavor; great in Swordfish Souvlaki (page 98).

- **Mantequilla, Spain:** Green; medium; remarkable fennel brine.

- **Cerignolas, Italy:** Black and green; huge, crisp sweet olives; just like mom used to put out at Thanksgiving, except with pits.

- **Niçoise, France:** Black; diminutive in size; a pleasant bite; perfect as a relish with fish or as a topping for pizza and of course, salad Niçoise (See Asparagus Niçoise, page 50).

(These olive reviews are from the website of my friend Suzanne Schmalzer, www.eatdrinkandbemarried.com.)

ond bowl. Mix all spices, sugar and salt in a bowl and sprinkle on the nuts. Toss to coat.

3. Spread the nut mixture in one layer on the baking sheet. Bake, shaking or stirring once, to make sure they roast evenly, 25 to 35 minutes, until they are crisp and browned. Transfer the nuts to another cool flat surface to cool and crisp.

 **VARIATION**

Curry Nuts Add 2 teaspoons curry powder to spice mix and proceed as above.

NOTE: If the nuts are not already toasted, place on a baking sheet in a single layer in a preheated 350°F (180°C) oven for 12 minutes.

SETTING UP A BUFFET

For anyone who doesn't have a caterer up their sleeve, a buffet is the most practical and flexible way to entertain. This is true for a number of reasons. Most important, you can prepare all of the food ahead of time and set it out before guests arrive. Guests can serve themselves, thereby sparing you the need to wait on them; as the host, you too are free to mingle. In the case of an open house, guests can come and go. Another plus—a buffet allows you to offer a more creative variety of dishes than would be practical at a seated meal. To make this into a foolproof entertaining solution there are some basic concepts I always try to keep in mind and some equipment I keep on hand.

THE EQUIPMENT

- A sturdy table, any size that will accommodate the food. If there is only one appropriate table for a buffet, allow the size of the table to set a limit on your menu.

- A cloth to cover the top of the buffet and two more that match for layering, fluffing and swagging.

- Two to four small, sturdy boxes of varying heights and sizes to use for creating levels on the tabletop. (Their looks don't matter; they will be covered with those two extra cloths. Mini milk crates are great.)

- If a warm dish is included in the menu, a chafing dish (for moist foods like stroganoff and chili) or a warming tray (for dry heat dishes like quiche and pizza) or both, plus a trivet or two. A fondue pot is fine for fondue or for keeping a sauce warm at the table. In a pinch, a slow cooker provides a homely but functional solution to keeping food warm on the buffet.

THE METHOD

A day (or two) before the party I place all of the serving platters, chafing dishes and bowls that will be required for my menu on the buffet. This allows me to take an inventory and make note of what's missing. I leave space on the table for a centerpiece (not necessarily in the center), plates, napkins and silverware. I take a moment in this peaceful pre-party time to arrange all of the elements on the table for ease of service and visual appeal. Plates are stacked where I plan for the buffet to begin. The traditional progression is to then place cold dishes and next warm dishes. Silverware and napkins are placed at the end. At this stage I use the sturdy boxes to add visual interest by placing them under some of the flat trays, bowls or hot tray to create a tiered effect. Chafing dishes and any platter that involves something guests will be cutting into are best resting securely on the table.

Once I've arranged the table to my liking, I remove the vessels and equipment and use the two extra cloths to cover the entire surface of the multi-level tabletop. The extra linens allow me to drape and scrunch the cloths around the levels to create an opulent, textured surface. Next I reposition the dishes and equipment and make final adjustments. At this point, I would also put each serving utensil in place to ensure I had them all. The centerpiece, whether a flower arrangement or a basket of red apples, could be positioned now, too. On the day of the party I tuck fresh flowers, leaves, whole nuts, grape clusters, miniature vegetables or whatever supports that party's theme, in and around the levels and serving dishes to finish off my lush, professional-looking buffet.

Salad Suggestions and Side Dishes

When you become a good cook, you become a good craftsman, first. You repeat and repeat and repeat until your hands know how to move without thinking about it.

—Jacques Pepin

IN THE 1980S, I ATTENDED a very fine cooking school in Paris, La Varenne Ecole de Cuisine. Often we were asked to prepare every possible variation on a recipe. For example, during one term we made ice cream in an astonishing array of flavors, all day long from almond to white chocolate and all of the fruits, for five straight days. By the end of that week I had learned how to make traditional French ice cream in a visceral way that will never leave me. In fact, some vestiges of that experience still cling to my thighs and upper arms.

The most challenging of these repetitive lessons took place during my first week of school. We spent five days entirely devoted to preparing variety meat—sweetbreads, tongue, brains, heart, kidney, tripe—the stuff most Americans don't eat. To make this week worse, I arrived as a long-time vegetarian. Somehow I hadn't made the connection beforehand: professional cooking school in France meant cooking "everything." With hindsight, I think this week was meant to cull the gourmands from the serious students.

At 1:30 on the first day we sat down to what became the daily ritual of lunch: First, taste the results of each other's cooking. Second, endure the chefs' comments about our results. Finally, eat until you were full (or, on some rare glorious occasions, until you were in a gluttonous daze). I quietly passed on everything offered to me. I thought I'd done my job by cooking the grisly body parts. I certainly wasn't going to eat any of it. The Chef de Cuisine corrected me in scathing, crisp French, *"Mange ou quitte"* ("Eat or get out"). I ate, I stayed.

That week I learned two lessons: how to prepare delicious sweetbreads, and that

SALAD COMBINATIONS PLUS DRESSING RECOMMENDATIONS

To make a good salad is to be a brilliant diplomatist—the problem is entirely the same in both cases. To know exactly how much oil one must put with one's vinegar.
—Oscar Wilde

It's difficult to think of anything but pleasant thoughts while eating a homegrown tomato.
—Lewis Grizzard

Most salads listed below can be transformed into entrées with the addition of the protein suggestions included.

GREENS AND VEGETABLE SALADS

An average serving is about 1 cup combined ingredients.

ASPARAGUS NIÇOISE Steamed asparagus, diced; cooked new potato; chopped scallions; and Niçoise olives with Cilantro Pesto (page 138), thinned with lemon juice and extra-virgin olive oil.

    Entrée option: Add smoked trout or Italian oil-packed tuna.

CHRISTMAS SALAD Baby spinach or arugula; walnuts; orange segments and pomegranate seeds with warmed Evan's Tangerine Vinaigrette (page 135).

you cannot cook well without tasting, repeating, correcting and tasting again. I also got a quick initiation into the deadly seriousness with which the French regard the preparation of food.

Another dish we prepared in a variety of ways until we knew the principle in our souls was the classic gratin. The section of gratins included in this chapter (starting on page 58) reflects that week. I had to practice to become a free, self-confident cook as I encourage you to do. Making a recipe until you *know* it is one of the essential strategies you need to become a confident host.

NEW WAVE SPINACH AND POMEGRANATE SALAD Spinach, watercress, cubed Macintosh apple, cubed avocado, toasted pecans and pomegranate seeds with Evan's Tangerine Vinaigrette (page 135).

PARIS BISTRO SALAD Sliced frisée; cooked, crumbled bacon or pancetta and toasted walnuts with Sherry Vinaigrette (page 133).
   Entrée option: Add cooked chicken, turkey or poached egg.

SOUTHWEST CAESAR SALAD Hearts of romaine with toasted pepitas, cherry tomatoes and roasted red pepper or poblano chile with Caesar Dressing (page 134).
   Entrée option: Add poached shrimp, chicken or grilled ahi.

PEAR, GORGONZOLA AND ARUGULA SALAD Arugula, sliced pear or fresh figs and crumbled Gorgonzola cheese with Sherry Vinaigrette (page 133).

BLACKBERRIES, PINE NUTS AND BRIE SALAD Endive, butter lettuce, blackberry, pine nuts and diced Brie with Evan's Tangerine Vinaigrette (page 135).

BABY GREENS WITH HERBS, WALNUTS AND FETA Baby greens, chopped fresh basil, walnuts or toasted pine nuts, dried cherries or cranberries and crumbled feta with Sherry Vinaigrette (page 133).
   Entrée option: Add poached salmon and fresh blueberries instead of dried fruit.

MUSHROOM SALAD WITH CANDIED ALMONDS Sliced cremini mushroom, grilled corn, Candied Almonds (page 43) and chives on butter lettuce with Roquefort Vinaigrette (page 133).

PROVENÇAL FENNEL SALAD Finely sliced fennel, orange segments, kalamata olives and sliced sweet onion with Evan's Tangerine Vinaigrette (page 135).
   Entrée option: Add grilled swordfish or sea bass.

GRILLED VEGETABLES WITH TAHINI Grilled eggplant, grilled zucchini and grilled portobello mushroom on watercress with Tahini-Lemon Vinaigrette (page 134).

SESAME GINGER COLESLAW Shredded cabbage, finely sliced white onion, toasted peanuts, diced pear or apple and chopped cilantro with Sesame-Ginger Mayonnaise (page 140) and a splash of seasoned rice vinegar.
Entrée option: Add poached shrimp or chicken.

ROASTED BEET AND BLUE CHEESE SALAD WITH CITRUS Diced, roasted beets; sliced pear; and crumbled blue cheese on watercress with Evan's Tangerine Vinaigrette (page 135).

POTATO, PASTA, RICE AND BEAN SALADS

An average serving is about ⅔ cup cooked potato, pasta, rice or beans plus the other ingredients.

BASIL NEW POTATO SALAD Steamed new potatoes; minced chives; chopped, hard-cooked eggs; minced celery; capers and diced red bell pepper with Basil Mayonnaise (page 140).
Entrée option: Add poached shrimp.

WHITE BEAN AND ALBACORE TUNA SALAD White beans, diced fennel, diced carrots, minced red onion and Italian oil-packed albacore or cooked shrimp with Tahini-Lemon Vinaigrette (page 134).

GREEN GRAPE AND CHICKEN TORTELLINI SALAD Chicken tortellini, green grapes, chopped scallions and pecan halves on watercress with Arugula Pesto (page 138).

SMOKED SALMON POTATO SALAD Steamed Yukon gold potatoes, minced red onion, minced dill and shredded smoked salmon with Lemon Parmesan Aïoli (page 139).

JASMINE RICE SALAD WITH SNOW PEAS AND GINGER Hot cooked jasmine rice tossed with Evan's Tangerine Vinaigrette (page 135). When cool, add snow peas, minced ginger, dried currants, diced red bell pepper, finely diced shallots and chopped cilantro.
Entrée option: Add diced ham or prosciutto.

CRAZY GUMBO SALAD Cooked rice, grilled shrimp, diced hard sausage, diced red and green bell peppers, chopped parsley, chopped scallions and ground coriander or sage with Arugula Pesto (page 138), diluted with chicken broth.

SHIITAKE MUSHROOM AND BOK CHOY PASTA SALAD Cooked rotelle pasta, sautéed shiitake mushrooms, diced bok choy, chopped green onion, diced red bell pepper, chopped fresh mint and pine nuts with Sesame-Ginger Mayonnaise (page 140).
Entrée option: Add cooked shrimp, turkey or chicken.

NICOLE'S TABBOULEH Cooked bulgur wheat, chopped cucumber, tomato and white onion, roasted red pepper and feta sprinkled with cumin seeds with Basil-Mint Pesto (page 138), thinned with lemon juice and olive oil.

Entrée option: Add sliced cooked lamb or chicken.

INDIAN CHICKEN SALAD Farfalle pasta with 3 tablespoons curry powder in the cooking water, red or green grapes, chopped poached chicken, chopped cilantro, toasted slivered almonds with Sesame-Ginger Mayonnaise (page 140).

FRUIT SALADS

When one has tasted watermelon he knows what the angels eat.

—Mark Twain

An average serving is about 1 cup combined fruit.

MEXICO CITY–STYLE JICAMA SALAD Sliced oranges, wedges of jicama and sliced tomatoes, sprinkled with cayenne pepper with Evan's Tangerine Dressing (page 135).

RUBY FRUIT SALAD Sliced strawberries and red plums tossed with chopped fresh basil, cinnamon and honey drizzled with crème fraîche or full-fat plain yogurt.

SUMMER MELON SALAD Cantalope, watermelon and casaba balls and chopped fresh mint drizzled with Midori liqueur.

TROPICAL FIESTA SALAD Pineapple, papaya, banana and toasted shredded coconut topped with diced candied ginger.

NECTARINE CHICKEN SALAD Sliced white nectarines or peaches; cooked, chopped chicken; diced celery and toasted walnuts on a bed of red leaf lettuce with Tahini-Lemon Vinaigrette (page 134).

RASPBERRY KUMQUAT SALAD Kumquat and raspberry tossed with honey, lime juice and minced ginger sprinkled with toasted sesame seeds.

GINGERY WALDORF SALAD Chopped Pippin apples, cubed Vermont Cheddar, walnuts, minced chives and seedless grapes with Sesame-Ginger Mayonnaise (page 140).

COINTREAU KIWIFRUIT SALAD Orange segments, kiwifruit slices, strawberry slices and cantalope wedges drizzled with Cointreau and sprinkled with poppy seeds.

Polenta with Wild Mushrooms and Walnuts

This recipe can be used for a soft cornmeal pudding or as an excellent alternate filling for the Stuffed Mushrooms on page 11. Polenta can also be chilled until firm and then grilled. To chill, transfer the polenta to a buttered 11 × 7-inch baking sheet and use a spatula to spread and smooth into an even layer. Chill at least one hour or until firm, then slice, lightly oil each side and crisp on a hot grill or under the broiler.

I often serve a grilled wedge of polenta on grilled radicchio, topped with currants, pine nuts, lemon zest and garlic bread crumbs as an elegant side dish with grilled fish.

Buffet • Quick and Easy • Inexpensive

PARTY TIME PREPARATIONS: Cook or reheat and serve.

SERVING EQUIPMENT: Serving bowl and large spoon.

Makes 8 servings

3 tablespoons unsalted butter	1 cup whipping cream
1 tablespoon olive oil	1/3 cup shredded Parmesan or Asiago cheese
1/2 cup finely minced onion	1/2 teaspoon ground white pepper
2 teaspoons minced garlic	2 teaspoons minced fresh rosemary
1 cup sliced shiitake mushrooms	1/2 cup walnuts, toasted (see note, page 45)
1 cup polenta or coarse ground cornmeal	
2 1/2 cups reduced-sodium or homemade chicken broth (see note, below)	

1. Heat 1 tablespoon of the butter and olive oil to bubbling in a heavy-bottom saucepan over medium heat. Add the onion and cook for 3 to 4 minutes. Add garlic and mushrooms; cook until softened and beginning to turn golden. Add the polenta and stir to mix. Slowly pour in the chicken broth, stirring constantly to blend. Raise heat to medium-high and whisk in the cream.

2. When well mixed, add all the remaining ingredients except the walnuts. Stirring constantly with a wooden spoon, cook for about 12 minutes, until the polenta becomes as thick as mashed potatoes. Taste and add salt and pepper as needed.

3. Remove from heat and stir in walnuts.

Polenta with Gorgonzola and Pine Nuts In Step 1, delete the mushrooms and proceed as above. In Step 3, instead of walnuts, stir in ⅓ cup crumbled Gorgonzola (or other good blue cheese) and ½ cup toasted pine nuts.

Pumpkin Polenta with Pecans In Steps 1 and 2, delete the mushrooms and rosemary and add instead 1 cup pumpkin puree, a pinch of cinnamon, ¾ teaspoon freshly grated nutmeg and ½ teaspoon dried thyme. In Step 3, instead of the walnuts, stir in ⅓ cup toasted pecan pieces. Garnish with fresh thyme sprigs.

NOTE: If you use unsalted homemade broth, add ½ teaspoon kosher salt.

OVEN-ROASTED VEGETABLES

The leap of faith required to commit your vegetables to a very hot oven introduces a whole new world of easily produced, complex flavors to your kitchen. Not only do these fire-roasted vegetables make wonderful side dishes, I use them to add intense flavor to soups and sauces. I was inspired by Barbara Kafka's fine book, *The Art of Roasting*.

Roasted vegetables on their own, or in combination with another roasted vegetable, need only light spicing to be complete side dishes—a sprinkle of cumin seeds or curry, soy sauce, lemon juice or minced garlic and a fresh herb like rosemary, thyme or cilantro.

Some of these vegetables seem like pretty obvious candidates for high-heat roasting such as potatoes and eggplant. The delicious surprises for me were the tender green vegetables like asparagus, scallions and green beans. And I have never liked zucchini so well as fire-roasted by this method and drizzled with lemon, thyme and grated Asiago cheese.

Basic Techniques:

- Preheat the oven to 500°F (260°C).

- Place all vegetables on a heavy sheet pan in one layer.

- Coat the surface of the vegetables generously with vegetable oil, olive oil or a mixture of 75 percent oil to 25 percent melted unsalted butter, unless "no oil" is indicated.

- A light sprinkle of kosher salt is always a good addition.

- Leave all vegetables whole, unless otherwise indicated.

- Turn all vegetables at least once during their indicated cooking time.

- All timing is approximate; look for a fully cooked vegetable. In the case of the eggplant or peppers, the skin will actually be blistered and blackened.

- To intensify flavors, during the last 10 minutes of roasting drizzle with infused oil, or oil to which you've added a fresh minced herb, garlic or ginger.

VEGETABLES REQUIRING 60 MINUTES OR LONGER

- Whole Large Eggplant (pricked, no oil): 1 hour or more. Scoop out the smoky-flavored flesh to use in sauces, salads, soups or spreads such as the Roasted Eggplant Spread (page 39).

VEGETABLES REQUIRING 40 TO 50 MINUTES

- Butternut Squash: (cut into 4 wedges, scrape out strings and seeds) 50 minutes.

- Sweet Potato: (peeled, sliced ¼ inch thick) 50 minutes. Drizzle with 50/50 mixture of maple syrup and orange juice or melted, unsalted butter with minced ginger and thyme for last 10 minutes.

- Small New Potato: (whole) 40 to 50 minutes. Toss with fresh, minced rosemary and crumbled Gorgonzola while warm or cool and combine with Basil Mayonnaise (page 140), roast garlic, onions, celery and red pepper for a roast potato salad.

- Idaho Potato: (cut lengthwise into 12 wedges each) 40 to 50 minutes. Add toasted cumin and cayenne to coating oil or sprinkle with malt vinegar and powdered garlic for last 5 minutes of roasting.

- Bell Peppers: (no oil, peel after roasting) 45 minutes. Slice and serve with wine vinegar, chopped parsley and walnuts or combine with roasted eggplant halves and zucchini for antipasto plate. Garnish the antipasto plate with capers, lemon peel and cured olives.

VEGETABLES REQUIRING 20 TO 30 MINUTES

- Carrots: (peeled and sliced ½ inch thick) 25 minutes. Drizzle with Evan's Tangerine Vinaigrette (page 135) or combine with red onion rings, chopped cilantro and pistachios.

- Red Onions: (sliced ¼ inch thick and separated into rings) 25 minutes.

- Garlic: (cut ¾ inch off the top of each head) 30 minutes. Add rosemary, thyme or basil to the oil and coat liberally. Put ½ inch broth or sherry in the bottom of the pan. Serve with Crostini (page 16) or add to any other roast vegetable dish, sauce or salad dressing.

- Zucchini: (sliced lengthwise ¼ inch thick) 30 minutes. Add lemon juice, minced thyme and grated Asiago cheese for last 5 minutes or sprinkle with black pepper and top with roasted cherry tomatoes.

- Spanish Onion: (cut lengthwise into 6 to 8 wedges) 30 minutes. Add 1 or 2 tablespoons of balsamic vinegar to the coating oil and rub in; combine with white beans, sage and prosciutto.

- Cherry Tomatoes: (whole) 25 minutes.

- Radicchio: (sliced in half) 20 minutes.

- Small Eggplant: (halved lengthwise, cook cut side down) 25 minutes. Drizzle with Tahini-Lemon Vinaigrette (page 134) or sprinkle with chopped sun-dried tomatoes, basil and mint.

- Asparagus: (tough stems removed) 10 to 12 minutes.
- Leeks: (quartered and sliced ¼ inch thick, well washed and dried) 10 to 15 minutes.
- Scallions: (sliced in half lengthwise) 10 to 15 minutes.
- Portobello or Shiitake Mushrooms: (wiped clean, stems removed, stem side down) 12 minutes. Add soy sauce or pureed garlic mixed into roasting oil. Sprinkle with minced thyme and lemon juice after roasting.

Potato Gratin with Forest Mushrooms

Gratins have always been one of my favorite side dishes for an elegant meal—especially in the winter and fall. Potato is the classic; the addition of mushrooms here introduces another layer of earthy goodness. The sweet potato variation, besides tasting mysteriously wonderful, is strikingly beautiful. Bright, springy colors jump out when you cut through the golden crust: apricot, yellow and spring green. The Sicilian-style variation is great with fish or to accompany juicy roast lamb.

Buffet • Completed in Advance

PARTY TIME PREPARATIONS: Can be assembled up to 1 day before and baked at party time, or the gratin may be completely baked the day before and reheated to serve.

SERVING EQUIPMENT: Dish in which it was baked, sharp knife and cake server.

Makes 10 servings

8 tablespoons (1 stick) unsalted butter

2 teaspoons minced garlic

1 pound fresh oyster or shiitake mushrooms, thinly sliced

2 teaspoons kosher salt

¼ cup dry white wine

2 cups whipping cream

2 tablespoons minced fresh thyme

½ teaspoon ground nutmeg

4 pounds Yukon Gold or russet potatoes, peeled and sliced ⅛ inch thick

1 cup chicken broth (low-sodium, if purchased)

¾ teaspoon freshly ground black pepper

1⅓ cups grated Fontina or Parmesan cheese

¾ cup fine bread crumbs

1. Preheat oven to 350°F (180°C). Butter a 4-quart casserole. In a large sauté pan, heat 3 tablespoons of the butter to sizzling. Add the garlic, mushrooms and 1 teaspoon of the salt. If you don't have a very large sauté pan, you may need to cook this in two batches. Sauté until the mushrooms are softened, about 5 minutes. Add white wine and simmer for 3 minutes longer. Add the cream, thyme and nutmeg. Bring to a simmer and let cook for 3 to 4 minutes, then remove from the heat and let cool.

2. Combine the cooled mushroom mixture, potatoes, chicken broth and remaining 1 teaspoon salt and pepper. Toss to mix and transfer half into the baking dish. Dot with half of the remaining butter. Add remaining potato mixture and top with remaining butter. Cover with buttered parchment paper and then foil and bake for 55 minutes.

3. Uncover, sprinkle on grated cheese and bread crumbs. Reduce heat to 325°F (165°C) and continue to bake for about 30 minutes, until the potatoes are tender, bubbling and golden. (Total baking time about 1½ hours.) Let rest 5 to 10 minutes before serving.

VARIATIONS

Festival Sweet Potato and Leek Replace the mushrooms with 1 pound of finely sliced and washed leeks, (white and tender green parts) and sauté as above in Step 1. Replace the white wine in Step 1 with cognac. Replace the potato with 3 pounds peeled sweet potatoes, sliced ⅛ inch thick. In Step 2, add 1 cup finely sliced dried nectarines or apricots. Complete as above.

Sicilian-Style Potato with Fennel In Step 1, add ¾ cup finely sliced onion into the pan along with 1½ tablespoons minced garlic. Replace the mushrooms with a combination of 2 pounds fennel bulbs (trimmed of fronds and thinly sliced, about 6 cups) and 1 thinly sliced, peeled large green apple. Sauté as above for 10 minutes, until soft. Replace the thyme with 1½ teaspoons fennel seeds and reduce the cream to 1½ cups. In Step 2, add ⅔ cup golden raisins. In Step 3, add ½ cup toasted pine nuts to the bread crumb and Fontina topping. Complete as above.

CORN ON THE COB

Fresh corn has a relatively long season, but never long enough for most of us. I like it any way I can get it, except overcooked. The easiest way to cook one or two ears is in the microwave. Wrap an ear and some fresh herbs in plastic wrap and cook for 3 minutes. Let cool a minute or two before unwrapping. For a party you need to steam, boil or grill a batch. I vastly prefer the grilled flavors. There are two successful approaches to grilling a batch of corn. The quickest is to strip off the husk and silk, brush the cob with butter and spices and wrap tightly in foil. The traditional style has you pull back the husks but leave them attached at the stalk, remove the silk, pull the leaves back up to cover and tie loosely with twine. Soak these in a bowl of water for 20 minutes (to keep the husks from burning up) before putting on a grill heated to low. The corn will take 12 to 15 minutes to cook if wrapped in foil and about 15 to 20 minutes in the soaked husks.

Couscous with Pistachios

Cold or hot, as a delicate side dish or as a filling cold salad for your next picnic, couscous is a wonderfully easy pasta to prepare. Its ricelike size makes it appealing in combination with other flavors and textures, and it is a nearly foolproof preparation—even for a novice.

Buffet • Quick and Easy • Vegetarian Option

PARTY TIME PREPARATIONS: Can be finished up to 1 day before and gently reheated at party time or served cold.

SERVING EQUIPMENT: If on a buffet, large bowl or platter and salad servers or large spoons.

Makes 8 servings

2½ cups water	3 cups couscous
2 cups chicken or vegetable broth	½ cup minced scallions
2 tablespoons olive oil or unsalted butter	¾ cup chopped pistachios, pine nuts or almonds
¼ teaspoon kosher salt	
¼ teaspoon freshly grated coarse black pepper	

1. In a medium saucepan, bring the water, broth, olive oil, salt and pepper just to a boil. Stir in the couscous and scallions and cover. Remove from the heat. Let rest off the heat 5 minutes; fluff with a fork.

2. Stir in the pistachios. Serve warm or at room temperature.

❋ VARIATIONS

Couscous with Kalamata and Orange In Step 1, add 1 tablespoon orange juice. In Step 2, stir in ½ cup chopped kalamata olives and 2 tablespoons grated orange zest with the pistachios. Season with salt and pepper to taste. Serve warm or at room temperature.

Cannellini, Prosciutto and Pesto Salad After Step 1, let the couscous cool. In Step 2, omit the pistachios and stir in 1 (15-ounce) can drained cannellini beans, 1 cup chopped scallions, ½ cup shredded prosciutto (about 2 ounces), ½ cup pesto or ½ cup shredded fresh oregano and 1 cup Evan's Tangerine Vinaigrette (page 135). Serve at room temperature or chilled.

Couscous with Mint, Feta and Fennel Prior to Step 1, finely slice one medium bulb fennel trimmed of fronds (about 1½ cups). Place in a microwave-safe container with 2 tablespoons water or chicken broth. Cover with plastic wrap and cook for 1 minute on High. Set aside to cool. Proceed with Step 1 as above.

Omit the pistachios in Step 2. Instead stir in ¼ cup chopped fresh mint, 1 cup crumbled feta cheese, ⅔ cup dried currants or cherries and the cooked fennel. Serve warm.

THE RULES OF RICE

Rice has been cultivated since at least 5,000 B.C. and grows in more than a hundred countries and on every continent except Antarctica. This has resulted in a staggering variety of rice and rice recipes; however, there are basically two kinds of rice: long grain and short grain.

Long grain rice has long, slender grains that cook separately. This kind of rice is frequently used for side dishes, entrées and casseroles. Long grain rices include basmati, Wehani, jasmine, Texmati, pecan and Carolina rice.

Short grain rice has a higher starch content than long grain rice and the small, round kernels stick together when cooked. Short grain rice is used in rice puddings and molds as well as for sushi. Classic short grain rices encompass risotto rices like Arborio and Carnaroli, as well as red rice, pudding rice and Japanese and Chinese rice.

Brown rice, which may be either short or long grain, has only the inedible outer husk removed. The high-fiber bran still covers the grain and provides the characteristic brown color and nutty flavor. White rice has the husk, bran and germ removed.

Methods for cooking rice vary so widely as to be overwhelming. Everyone I know has a "secret" to perfect rice, and none of them are the same. I'll tell you my secret: a rice cooker. They are widely available, relatively inexpensive and guarantee a perfect product. Rice and water are placed in the cooker according to the manufacturer's directions and off it goes. Ten to fifteen minutes later you have perfectly cooked rice, which the cooker will keep warm until needed. Fluff the rice with a fork or slotted spoon before serving.

If you do not own a rice cooker, rice can be cooked in a heavy pot on the stovetop. The proportion of long grain rice to liquid is about 1½ cups rice to 2¼ cups broth or water. Short grain rice proportions are generally 1½ cup rice to 2½ cups water. Combine all ingredients in a pot along with some salt and possibly some butter, bring to a boil and cook over low heat approximately 20 minutes. Brown rice will take about 40 minutes. Risotto rice, long a favorite in Italian cuisine, is cooked differently than other short grain rices, and it is best to follow directions on the package.

Golden Mashed Potatoes

Mashed potatoes are a great choice for a menu for entertaining. They are one of the few dishes you can feel certain will appeal to everyone from kids to grandparents. The classic is updated here with the use of silky Yukon Gold potatoes; while not as fluffy as the traditional russet, their name is well deserved. They are as good as gold with a creamy flesh that tastes as if butter had been injected on the vine.

Quick and Easy • Inexpensive • Kid Appeal

PARTY TIME PREPARATIONS: Heat and serve.

SERVING EQUIPMENT: Serving bowl and serving spoon.

Makes 8 servings

4 pounds Yukon Gold potatoes	1 teaspoon kosher salt, or to taste
5 to 8 tablespoons unsalted butter, softened	¼ teaspoon white or black pepper, or to taste
¾ cup whipping cream or milk	

1. Wash the potatoes and prick all over with a knife. Put in the microwave on a paper towel and cook on High for 15 to 20 minutes, turning them over after 10 minutes. Cook until the potatoes are tender without being mushy; a sharp knife should slip easily into the centers.

2. Cool the potatoes enough to handle and peel. Cut the potatoes into a rough dice and put in the bowl of an electric mixer. Whip on low, adding the butter, 1 tablespoon at a time. (If you prefer really creamy mashed potatoes, put them through a ricer or press through the screen of a strainer before putting into the mixer.)

3. Warm the cream in the microwave for 20 seconds on High. Once the butter is incorporated into the potatoes, slowly add the warm cream with the mixer running. You may add up to 3 tablespoons more butter at this stage if you prefer a really buttery flavor. Season with salt and pepper.

4. Serve the mashed potatoes immediately or keep warm in a tightly covered, buttered casserole in a 200°F (95°C) oven for up to 1 hour. To hold until the next day, let the potatoes cool to room temperature, cover tightly with plastic wrap and refrigerate. To reheat: About an hour before serving, remove potatoes from the refrigerator. Brush the top with melted butter and add 1 tablespoon cream or milk. Cover with a paper towel and heat in the microwave for 45 to 60 seconds on High.

Remove towel and stir to blend. Replace paper towel and heat for 20 to 30 seconds or until hot.

✻ VARIATIONS

Wasabi Mashed Potatoes Add ½ cup chopped scallions and 2 tablespoons wasabi powder (a Japanese horseradish available in the spice section of the supermarket or Asian grocery stores) to potatoes after the cream is incorporated in Step 3.

Goat Cheese Mashed Potatoes Add ½ cup minced shallots to the cream while heating in Step 3. Add 6 to 8 ounces room-temperature goat cheese, like Montrachet, into the mixer along with the cream in Step 3.

Mashed Potatoes Pommery Add 3 tablespoons whole-grain mustard, like Pommery, along with the cream in Step 3.

Mashed Sweet Potatoes and Parsnips Replace the potatoes with 2 pounds sweet potatoes and 2 pounds parsnips. Peel the vegetables and trim the ends from the parsnips. Cut both vegetables into 1½-inch discs. Instead of Step 1, steam the sweet potatoes and parsnips over boiling water until easily pierced with a knife tip, about 12 minutes for the sweet potatoes and 17 minutes for the parsnips. When cool enough to handle, proceed as above in Step 2, but add 1 tablespoon brown sugar and ¼ teaspoon ground allspice or nutmeg. Finish as above in Step 3.

It's a nice finishing touch to top each serving with the Candied Nuts (page 43).

ONE POTATO, TWO POTATO

Potatoes can be broken into two general categories: low starch and high starch. Low-starch potatoes tend to have wetter, denser meat when cooked; therefore, they are the ideal choice when you need a cooked spud to hold its shape for presentation. Fingerlings, round whites, round reds and new potatoes are low-starch potatoes. These are great in a gratin, potato salads, smashed potato or oven-roasted whole. Russet potatoes are high-starch potatoes and characteristically are drier and flourlike when cooked. Perfect for baking, frying and mashing, high-starch potatoes will yield fluffy, airy results (see Golden Mashed Potatoes on page 63).

Quick Bean Dishes

These quick recipes are based on the use of premium-quality canned beans. The addition of fresh herbs and spices can make canned beans into a satisfying side dish to enliven a plate of simple grilled fish or meat. The Frijoles Ranchero are great with grilled swordfish and corn on the cob. Fagioli al Pesto complements both the Arugula Pesto Roast Lamb (page 81) and the Roast Chicken with Shiitake Mushrooms (page 93). Turkish Spiced Chickpeas would make a lovely side dish for the Lamb Burgers (page 112). Caribbean Black Beans with Thyme would be an easy hit alongside roasted salmon.

The recipes can also be used as the springboard for other legume dishes. By increasing the proportion of vegetable to beans you can easily turn one of these into a bean salad. The addition of proteins like cubed cheese or ham, poached chicken or shrimp turns these into easy main dishes for a summer luncheon or picnic.

Quick and Easy • Inexpensive • Healthy

PARTY TIME PREPARATIONS: Heat and serve.

SERVING EQUIPMENT: Bowl or deep platter and serving spoon.

Makes 8 servings

FRIJOLES RANCHERO

¾ cup chicken or beef broth

1 teaspoon minced garlic

Juice of 2 limes

¼ teaspoon ground cumin or 1 tablespoon minced fresh oregano

1 cup diced, peeled tomato

3 (15-ounce) cans pinto beans, drained

Kosher salt and freshly ground coarse black pepper, to taste

1 serrano or jalapeño chile, seeded and minced (optional)

2 tablespoons tequila (optional)

½ cup chopped fresh cilantro or Italian parsley

1. Bring the broth, garlic, lime juice and cumin to a simmer. Reduce the heat to low and add the tomato and beans. Heat through. Taste for salt and pepper.
2. Stir in the chile and tequila, if using, and serve topped with the chopped cilantro.

Fagioli al Pesto

½ cup chicken or vegetable broth

2 tablespoons dry vermouth

3 (15-ounce) cans Great Northern white beans, drained

⅓ cup Basil Pesto (page 136) or purchased

1 tablespoon grated lemon zest

Kosher salt and freshly ground coarse black pepper, to taste

¼ cup shredded prosciutto or ½ cup shaved Parmigiano-Reggiano cheese

1. Puree all of the ingredients, except the prosciutto, in a food processor until creamy.
2. Place the puree in a microwave-safe container. Heat in the microwave on High for 2 to 3 minutes, until bubbling. Top with the prosciutto and serve.

Turkish Spiced Chickpeas

3 (15-ounce) cans garbanzo beans, drained

½ cup chicken or vegetable broth

½ teaspoon ground cayenne pepper

1 tablespoon pureed garlic

2 tablespoons fresh lemon juice

1 bunch scallions (white and green parts), cut into ¼-inch dice

Kosher salt and freshly ground coarse black pepper, to taste

¼ cup chopped fresh parsley or mint or 2 tablespoons chopped fresh oregano

4 ounces feta cheese, crumbled (optional)

¼ cup pitted kalamata or Niçoise olives (optional)

1. Puree half of the beans in a blender or food processor.
2. Combine the broth, cayenne, garlic, pureed beans and lemon juice in a microwave-safe container. Heat in the microwave on High for 1½ minutes, until bubbling. Stir in the remaining beans and scallions. (The dish can be completed to this step and stored in the refrigerator for up to 24 hours.) Heat on High for 1 minute, stir and continue to heat and stir, in 1-minute increments, until the beans are piping hot. Stir in the parsley. Season with salt and pepper. Top with the cheese and olives (if using) and serve.

Caribbean Black Beans with Thyme

½ cup chicken or vegetable broth

2 tablespoons minced shallot

1 teaspoon ground coriander or cardamom

2 tablespoons minced fresh thyme

1 tablespoon grated orange zest

2 tablespoons dry sherry or Madeira

2 tablespoons orange juice

½ cup chopped dried apples (optional)

3 (15-ounce) cans black beans, drained

1. Combine all the ingredients, including the dried apples, if using, except the beans in a saucepan over medium-low heat and cover. Simmer gently for 5 minutes to blend the flavors.
2. Add the beans and simmer for 4 to 5 minutes to heat through.

STEAMED VEGETABLES

Steaming is one of the simplest methods of vegetable preparation. If done correctly, leaving the vegetables crisp-tender, it is one of the surest ways to reveal the natural flavor of the vegetable itself. Perfectly steamed broccoli, asparagus or sugar snap peas need just a dot of butter, a spritz of lemon juice and a pinch of salt to accompany a rich or complex entrée.

An inexpensive steamer basket, nestled into a larger pot, or an ultra-convenient electric steamer, are the best ways to prepare steamed vegetables for a crowd. If using the steamer basket, be careful to keep the water line below the bottom of the basket; make sure the lid fits tightly on the pan and do not overload the pan. Also keep in mind that if you try to steam too many vegetables at once they will cook unevenly from top to bottom. For small quantities I find the microwave a cleaner, quicker method. When I steam in the microwave I add 1 to 2 tablespoons broth to the dish with the vegetables and cover loosely with plastic wrap.

All large vegetables should be cut into chunks before steaming. Times below are for vegetables placed over already steaming water. Cooking times necessarily vary due to differences in sizes and maturity of particular vegetables. The times are only a guideline. Vegetables should be tested with the tip of a knife for tenderness.

QUICK (3 TO 6 MINUTES)

- Asparagus
- Haricots verts
- Green beans
- Mushrooms

- Spinach
- Peas
- Sugar snap peas
- Snow peas

MODERATE (6 TO 8 MINUTES)

- Baby carrots
- Broccoli
- Cauliflower

- Summer squash
- Baby bok choy
- New potatoes

LONGEST (20 TO 30 MINUTES)

- Beets
- Brussels sprouts
- Cabbage
- Large carrots
- Corn on the cob
- Greens

- Leeks
- Pearl onions
- Potatoes
- Winter squash
- Yams

Grilled Vegetables

Summer cooking implies a sense of immediacy, a capacity to capture the fleeting moment.

—Elizabeth David

All vegetables benefit from a light coating of vinaigrette or olive oil, herbs, salt and pepper for an hour or two before grilling. All vegetables are turned once halfway through the cooking time indicated, unless they are marked with an asterisk. The asterisk indicates they should be turned several times.

	CUT, SIZE OR SHAPE	GRILL TEMPERATURE	COOKING TIME	FLAVOR ADDITIONS
Asparagus	Woody stems removed	Medium-high	5 to 6 minutes	Lemon zest, sesame seeds
Bell peppers*	Halved lengthwise	Medium	10 to 12 minutes	Garlic, basil
Carrots	¼ inch thick, cut on diagonal	Medium-high	10 minutes	Fennel, cumin, ginger, brown sugar, cardamom
Cauliflower	Sliced horizontally into large, ½-inch thick discs	Medium-high	12 to 15 minutes	Cumin, curry, ginger, thyme
Eggplant	Japanese: halved lengthwise Globe: cut in ¾-inch slices	Medium-high	8 to 10 minutes	Garlic, cayenne
Garlic	Whole, top sliced off, drizzled with olive oil and wrapped in foil	Low	30 to 40 minutes	Olive oil, thyme, rosemary, oregano
Large mushrooms	Whole, stems removed	Medium-high	8 to 10 minutes	Chervil, marjoram, parsley, cayenne, basil, shallot
Potatoes (small)	Whole if under 1½ inch in diameter, or halved	Medium	10 to 15 minutes	Basil, chives, garlic, paprika, thyme
Radicchio and endive	Whole	Medium-low	5 to 6 minutes	Garlic, oregano, balsamic vinegar
Scallions	Whole, trimmed of roots and long tops	Medium-high	4 minutes	Thyme
Turnips	Peeled, sliced into ¼-inch discs	Medium	10 to 12 minutes	Garlic, thyme, parsley
Zucchini	Halved lengthwise	Medium	8 to 10 minutes	Thyme, rosemary, garlic

Entrées

Burgundy makes you think of silly things; Bordeaux makes you talk about them, and Champagne makes you do them.

—Jean Anthelme Brillat-Savarin

FRESH OUT OF COOKING SCHOOL I went to work for a wealthy family in the Normandy region of France. They enjoyed hosting a perpetual flurry of parties for which they expected me to produce sophisticated food. At the conclusion of one particularly demanding soiree, I heaved a sigh of relief as I served dessert, a beautiful frangipane and pear tarte. I could now retreat to my bedroom, have a glass of sherry and pass out. As I turned to leave, the host caught my eye and indicated that he'd like me to sit down at the table. "Nicole, please join us. I am serving a very special Sauterne to go with your beautiful pear tarte, a Chateau d'Yquem."

I had never had a Sauterne, or any "sweet" wine for that matter, that I cared for. In my ignorance, I said as much. There was a hushed silence of gourmands in shock. I am indebted to my employer for overlooking my gaucherie and insisting that I try some, "Just this once." It turned out that the combination of Chateau d'Yquem and ripe pear is justifiably famous. The syrupy, lightly floral wine made the pears evanesce to perfume in my mouth. On average, only five thousand bottles of this lovely wine are produced in a good year; it was a rare and special treat.

This was my first experience with the magic that can be created by the perfect pairing of wine and food. That is why every hors d'oeuvre, entrée and dessert recipe in this book includes a suggestion for a complementary wine.

There are many other famous parings: Stilton with port, foie gras and late harvest Riesling, chocolate with port, Muscadet and oysters, biscotti and Vin Santo and Pinot Noir with salmon. Not all combinations produce such a seductive synergy as these, but serving the right beverage will always make your food taste better and elevate your guests' experience of the meal.

When I plan a party menu I always begin with the selection of an entrée that suits the occasion. I then have a focus that makes selecting the rest of the menu easier. This chapter includes main courses that address every style of entertaining from a Super Bowl bash to a romantic soiree for two. Utilize the descriptive phrases at the beginning of each recipe to help you make the best selection for your event. And, of course, you'll find complementary wines indicated as well.

TABLES OF CONTENT

Take time to plan how you'd like your dining table to look long before you're ready to send out invitations. I've found that a great tablecloth, one that really goes with my dining room, is the easiest way to set the tone for the rest of the tabletop. You're way ahead of the party if you buy two or three table linens that are appropriate for all seasons and occasions.

Once you have your linens, seek out a vase that complements each cloth, napkins, napkin wrappers (not necessarily "rings") and place card holders (could be anything from formal crystal holders to tiny wind-up toys). The option of creating a table all in shades of one color makes the process easier, and it can be a very dramatic look.

Once you've found a vase or two that work with your cloths, figure out what flowers (by season) set well in each vase. Collect seasonal tabletop decorations that you can store for special-occasion entertaining. I have a basket of dried baby corn, tiny dried squashes and ceramic pomegranates that I use in the fall. I store seashells, coral and small beach toys in a child's beach pail, which becomes part of a summer tabletop.

When you're deciding on the settings for your table there are three very different looks that can be equally successful depending on the type of party. One is the traditional approach of purchasing matching sets of 8 to 12 of everything. However, a table for a less formal affair can also look perfect with mismatched glasses or plates or napkins as long as any two of those three elements *do* match.

To master the mismatched look, build a collection of dishes or glasses or napkins that have some common theme that ties them together: Fiesta Ware, blue glass, white lace. My friend and writing coach Suzanne collects white dishes from a variety of designers and eras so no matter how she combines her collection, it looks planned. This creates a lively, festive look for a party table, while also being easy on the pocketbook. As a rule of thumb, only one main element of your table setting should be mismatched.

The third option, effective for a casual or theme party, is a completely mismatched table setting. In this case, each piece can be unique as long as a single color (purple), texture (like bamboo) or pattern (let's say different florals) ties them together.

Roast Tenderloin of Beef with Horseradish-Dijon Butter

A tenderloin of beef is the hands-down favorite of my friends and clients for any festive occasion. It is the most tender and flavorful cut of beef and needs little more than some herbs, garlic and a quick roasting in high heat. Some things are so good on their own I hesitate to gussy them up, but I have included a variety of compound butters (page 145) to serve with the beef, lending this preparation all the variety it needs. Compound butters are ideal for entertaining because they can be prepared days in advance and then spooned on the roast meat to melt into a shiny, luscious sauce.

Formal • Quick and Easy • Pricey

PARTY TIME PREPARATIONS: Roast and serve.

SERVING EQUIPMENT: If served on a buffet, a cutting board, carving set and small knife for compound butter.

BEVERAGE TO ACCOMPANY: Cabernet Sauvignon

Makes 8 servings

HORSERADISH-DIJON BUTTER

8 tablespoons (1 stick) unsalted butter, creamed

2 tablespoons minced shallot

1 tablespoon minced chives

1 tablespoon Dijon mustard

1 teaspoon prepared horseradish

ROAST TENDERLOIN OF BEEF

4-pound, center-cut, USDA prime beef fillet, rolled and tied by the butcher, leaving about ¼ inch fat

1½ tablespoons minced garlic

2 teaspoons minced thyme

1 teaspoon minced fresh rosemary

1 tablespoon kosher salt

1½ teaspoons freshly ground coarse black pepper

2 tablespoons olive oil

1. **TO MAKE THE BUTTER:** Combine all of the ingredients in a food processor and pulse to blend thoroughly. Transfer the butter to a sheet of waxed paper or plastic wrap and form into a 1-inch-diameter log. Wrap tightly and refrigerate. This can be prepared up to 3 days before use.
2. Cut shallow slits along the top or fat side of the roast. Mix the garlic, thyme, rosemary, salt and pepper and rub into the slits and all over the roast. Let rest at room temperature for 1 hour. Drizzle the olive oil all over the top of the roast.

3. Preheat the oven to 450°F (230°C). Put the roast on an ungreased, shallow roasting pan. Roast for 24 minutes. Check the temperature of the roast with an instant-read thermometer. When the center of the roast registers 120°F (50°C) for rare or 125 to 130°F (50 to 55°C) for medium rare, remove from the oven. (Total cooking time will be 30 to 40 minutes.) Let rest for at least 10 minutes before carving.

4. Slice the beef ½ inch thick and top each serving with a ¼-inch wedge of the compound butter.

▨ VARIATION

Blue Cheese Butter Replace the Dijon mustard with 3 tablespoons crumbled Roquefort or other good blue cheese.

SALT SAVVY

Once traded at the same souks with myrrh and frankincense, salt has historically been a valuable commodity. Recently, however, we have uncritically shaken fine-grained iodized salt out of the familiar round container and given it hardly a thought. Then, about five years ago, sea salts starting turning up in gourmet stores and on fancy restaurant menus. These days, one of the most common questions asked in my cooking classes is, "What's the difference between sea salt, table salt and kosher salt? Which is better?"

The short answer to this question is the following:

- Table Salt: Ground and refined rock salt with an anticaking agent and often iodine.
- Kosher Salt: Refined rock salt without additives and larger grains than table salt.
- Sea Salt: Evaporated directly from the sea. Typically in a very large grain with the mineral or briny flavors of the sea from which it was harvested. Designer sea salts can be found in gourmet stores, and can be very pricey. Fleur de sel with its slightly sweet, floral flavor and sel gris, a gray salt with a pronounced mineral flavor, are two of the most available sea salts.

I find kosher salt preferable for all cooking for two reasons: it doesn't have any of the metallic flavor of table salt and the larger grains are easier to control when adding a "pinch." I offer beautiful sea salt on the table for guests to add at their discretion. I do not use table salt at all.

Pork Tenderloin with Fig Sauce

The spice rub adds flavor to the meat and the simple fig sauce creates a dish elegant enough for any party. I serve this with the slices of pork and sauce fanned over the Provençal Fennel Salad (page 51). The combination of tender meat, sweet sauce and crunchy fennel is a hands-down favorite in all of my cooking classes and great for any spring or summer party.

The first variation introduces a fantastic, made-ahead Balsamic Blueberry Sauce that would be equally good on chicken, duck, turkey or pork. The second variation uses these same bright flavors on a turkey roast.

Casual • Formal • Quick and Easy

PARTY TIME PREPARATIONS: Can be prepared the night before and baked after guests arrive.

SERVING EQUIPMENT: Serving platter and carving utensils.

BEVERAGE TO ACCOMPANY: Gewürztraminer, Riesling or Viognier

Makes 8 servings

FIG SAUCE
1 cup chicken stock

3 tablespoons sherry

1 teaspoon balsamic vinegar

⅔ cup diced dried Calimyrna figs

1 orange, peeled, segmented and chopped, juice reserved

2 tablespoons honey

¼ teaspoon toasted cumin seeds

⅓ cup packed light brown sugar

Pinch ground cinnamon

Kosher salt and white pepper, to taste

DRY RUB
1 teaspoon minced dried thyme

1 teaspoon cayenne pepper

1 teaspoon ground sage

1 tablespoon garlic powder or granulated garlic

1 teaspoon crushed fennel seeds

1 tablespoon kosher salt

1 tablespoon coarsely ground black pepper

PORK TENDERLOIN
¼ cup olive oil

3 (1- to 1¼-pound) pork tenderloins

TO SERVE
Provençal Fennel Salad

1. **TO MAKE THE SAUCE:** Combine all of the ingredients in a saucepan and cook over medium heat, stirring often, until the sugar is melted and the figs have softened, 12 to 15 minutes. Use a handheld immersion blender or transfer to a food processor to puree the sauce; there will still be chunks. Set aside. (This could be prepared up to 2 days ahead.)

2. **TO MAKE THE DRY RUB:** Combine all the ingredients in a small bowl.

3. Brush half of the oil all over the pork; liberally coat with the rub, using your hands to rub it in. Let the meat rest at room temperature for 2 hours or overnight in the refrigerator. If it has been refrigerated, bring out to warm for 30 minutes before cooking.

4. Preheat the oven to 350°F (180°C). Fold over the small tail ends of each tenderloin and tie with kitchen twine so that each piece of meat is of a more or less even diameter from end to end.

5. Add the remaining oil to a large roasting pan over high heat. When the oil is hot, add the tied tenderloins and use tongs to turn and brown evenly on all sides, 3 to 4 minutes.

6. Pour the Fig Sauce over the meat, turning the meat to coat well. Roast for 20 minutes, until an instant-read thermometer registers 140 to 145°F (60 to 65°C). Baste several times with the pan sauce.

7. Remove the tenderloins to a platter, cover with foil and let rest for 5 minutes before carving into ½-inch slices. Reduce the pan sauce if desired. Serve the pork slices on the salad drizzled with the sauce.

❈ VARIATIONS

Omit the Provençal Fennel Salad, marinate and roast the pork without the Fig Sauce. Prepare the following to serve over the cooked pork.

Balsamic Blueberry Sauce

¼ cup plus 3 to 4 tablespoons unsalted butter

½ cup minced shallots

1½ cups chicken broth

1 cup balsamic vinegar

2 tablespoons grated orange zest

1 cup fresh or frozen blueberries or blackberries

2 teaspoons minced chipotle chiles in adobo (optional)

1. Melt the ¼ cup butter in a heavy saucepan over medium heat. Add the shallots and sauté until soft, about 5 minutes. Add the chicken broth and increase the heat to high. Boil until reduced by half, 7 to 8 minutes. Add the balsamic vinegar and boil until reduced to about 1¼ cups.

2. Reduce the heat to low and stir in the orange zest and blueberries and chiles, if using. Let the sauce simmer gently for 4 to 5 minutes to blend the flavors and

slightly cook the fruit. (The sauce can be made to here up to 24 hours in advance.) When you are ready to serve the sauce, place over low heat and stir in the remaining butter, a chunk at a time.

Turkey Roast with Fig Sauce. Replace the pork tenderloin with a rolled, boneless, 3- to 4-pound turkey breast. Skip Step 4. Roast at 400°F (205°C) for about 1 hour, until the roast reaches an internal temperature of 145 to 150°F (65°C). Complete as above.

The Wellington Concept

Classic and impressive beef Wellington was the inspiration for this group of easy, individually wrapped entrées. Puff pastry encloses tender cuts of salmon, lamb and beef, each complemented by exciting herbs. It is a main course fit for special occasions and is often thought to take a great deal of time and skill to make. However, this nontraditional version of the dish, utilizing purchased puff pastry, is quick and accessible to any home cook. The bundles can be prepared up to a week in advance, frozen and popped in the oven at party time. One of the things to remember about puff pastry is that it must be cold (but not frozen) when placed into a hot oven in order for the pastry to become light and flaky. A very simple green vegetable on the side is all you need for a completely beautiful party plate.

Formal • Completed in Advance

PARTY TIME PREPARATIONS: Bake and serve.

SERVING EQUIPMENT: If served on a buffet, a large, flat platter and serving spatula.

BEVERAGE TO ACCOMPANY: Pinot Noir, Cabernet Franc, Sangiovese

Makes 8 servings

SALMON WITH SPINACH AND FETA IN PUFF PASTRY

2 tablespoons unsalted butter

3 tablespoons minced shallots

1 cup thawed, well-drained, frozen spinach

¼ teaspoon ground nutmeg

1 tablespoon grated lemon zest

2 teaspoons minced fresh thyme or dill

Kosher salt and freshly ground coarse black pepper, to taste

3 tablespoons crumbled feta cheese

8 thick, skinless fillets of salmon (about 6 ounces each)

4 (17-ounce) packages puff pastry, thawed in refrigerator

1 egg, lightly beaten with 1 teaspoon milk

1. Heat a sauté pan with the butter over medium heat. Add the shallots and sauté 3 to 4 minutes, until softened. Reduce the heat to medium-low and add the spinach, nutmeg, lemon zest, thyme, salt and pepper. Sauté for 2 to 3 minutes to blend. Remove the pan from the heat and stir in the feta. Taste for seasoning and let cool.

2. Lightly salt and pepper each piece of salmon and top with 2 tablespoons of the spinach mixture.

3. Roll out pastry sheets on a lightly floured board. For each fillet, cut 1 piece of pastry for the bottom about 1 inch larger than the salmon and 1 piece large enough to drape over the fillet and touch the countertop, plus 1 inch to spare all the way around.

4. Brush the edge of the smaller sheet with the egg mixture. Place a piece of salmon on the center of the pastry. Drape the larger piece over the salmon and seal the two pieces of dough together by folding the edges over once and pleating like a pie crust. Repeat for each "package." Chill for at least 30 minutes or freeze for up to 1 week before baking.

5. Preheat the oven to 425°F (220°C). Brush the top of each package with a little of the egg mixture. Put on a baking sheet lined with parchment paper and a dusting of cornmeal. Bake for 18 to 23 minutes, until golden. Let rest 5 to 10 minutes before serving.

▨ VARIATIONS

Beef Wellington with Gorgonzola and Mushrooms Replace the salmon with 8 (5- to 6-ounce) beef fillets, about 2 inches thick. Skip Steps 1 and 2. Season the fillets with salt and pepper and sear on all sides in a very hot pan, 3 to 4 minutes. Let cool, then proceed with the recipe in Step 3. Once the beef is sitting on the bottom pastry sheet, top each fillet with ½ teaspoon horseradish sauce, 1 to 2 tablespoons crumbled Gorgonzola or Roquefort cheese and 1 to 2 tablespoons sautéed mushrooms. Press the toppings gently to flatten on to the beef. Complete and bake as above.

Lamb with Pesto in Puff Pastry Replace the salmon with 8 (4- to 5-ounce) lamb noisettes (cut from the loin or rib), about 2 inches thick. Skip Steps 1 and 2. Season the noisettes with salt and pepper and sear on all sides in a very hot pan, 3 to 4 minutes. Top each noisette with 1 to 2 tablespoons of Basil-Mint Pesto (page 138), and chopped pistachios. Complete and bake as above starting in Step 3.

Arugula Pesto Roast Lamb

You can prepare this lamb the day before your party and just pop it in the oven to roast as guests arrive. My friend Denise Vivaldo suggested the use of prepared pesto to create this easy, easy party roast. Arugula and orange peel are Mediterranean flavors that stand up well to the flavorful lamb. The variation with cilantro and lime has a very Southwestern feel and is great served with the Caribbean Black Beans with Thyme (page 66), grilled corn on the cob and warm tortillas or naan.

Casual • Formal • Quick and Easy

PARTY TIME PREPARATIONS: Bake and serve.

SERVING EQUIPMENT: If served on a buffet, add a deep platter and include a large fork or tongs for serving.

BEVERAGE TO ACCOMPANY: Shiraz, Barolo, Cabernet Sauvignon

Makes 8 to 10 servings

1 (about 4 pounds) butterflied, boned leg of lamb

Kosher salt and freshly ground coarse black pepper, to taste

1 recipe Arugula Pesto (page 138) or 1 (7-ounce) container pesto

Peel of 1 orange, all white pith removed and sliced into matchsticks

1 tablespoon olive oil

1. Preheat the oven to 400°F (205°C). Oil the bottom of a 9 × 13-inch baking dish.
2. Unfold the lamb, fat side down, on a clean work surface. Sprinkle with salt and pepper. Spread the entire amount of pesto over the lamb, rubbing it in. Sprinkle the orange strips across the meat. Fold the lamb back up to resemble the way the butcher gave it to you. Truss with kitchen twine or netting. Rub the roast with the olive oil. Lightly salt and pepper the outside of the roast.
3. Place the lamb in the prepared baking dish. Bake for 50 to 70 minutes, depending on desired doneness (remove at 125°F [50°C] for rare, or 135°F [55°C] for medium-rare). Let sit for 10 minutes before slicing. Using a carving knife, slice diagonally into ¼-inch-thick slices.

✺ VARIATIONS

Cilantro Lime Roast Lamb Replace the Arugula Pesto with the Cilantro Pesto (including the optional minced chile) on page 138. Replace the orange peel with the peel from 2 limes (all white pith removed), sliced into matchsticks. Finish as above.

Basil-Mint Kalamata Roast Lamb Replace the Arugula Pesto with the Basil-Mint Pesto (page 138) and replace the orange peel with ½ cup chopped kalamata olives. Finish as above.

TAKING STOCK

Stock to a cook is voice to a singer.

—Anonymous

Most soup recipes call for stock where water might perform as well. But flavorful stock or broth, whether it is chicken, beef, fish or vegetable, gives soup backbone and a richness that water cannot impart. Making stock from scratch is easy, requiring nothing but time and the best available ingredients. If you do not have the time, don't worry. There are several excellent-quality stocks available in grocery stores. Whenever possible buy the low- or reduced-sodium prepared stock to avoid the risk of over salting a soup or sauce as it reduces. The most successful products are sold as a liquid in resealable aseptic packages (like soy milk), or as a very reduced concentrate or paste. These are superior to the products in aluminum cans that can impart a metallic taste once exposed to air.

Braised Beef Short Ribs with Mushroom-Thyme Sauce

Simple preparation and slow cooking turn this humble cut of meat into a complexly flavored, tender treat suitable for an elegant dinner party. This heartwarming winter dish can be completed up to two days before serving. As it cooks, the liquid ingredients become a luscious sauce. The robustly flavored Cuban variation is perfect served with black beans and rice.

For a beautiful plate, stand the short ribs upright in polenta with chives or pappardelle tossed with parsley and Niçoise olives. Sprinkle the gremolata over all.

Formal • Completed in Advance

PARTY TIME PREPARATIONS: Bake and serve or reheat and serve.

SERVING EQUIPMENT: If on a buffet, a chafing dish and large spoon.

BEVERAGE TO ACCOMPANY: Cabernet Sauvignon, Petit Syrah, Merlot

Makes 8 to 10 entrée servings

SHORT RIBS

7 to 8 pounds beef short ribs, cut into 3½ × 2-inch pieces (approximately 24 ribs)

2 teaspoons kosher salt

2 teaspoons freshly ground coarse black pepper

½ cup all-purpose flour

1½ tablespoons fennel seeds

½ cup olive oil

4 cups finely sliced yellow onions

⅓ cup minced garlic

4 cups sliced cremini or porcini mushrooms (about ¾ pound)

2 cups beef broth

1½ cups chopped canned tomatoes

2 tablespoons tomato paste

3 bay leaves

¼ teaspoon ground cinnamon

2 tablespoons chopped fresh thyme

¼ cup orange juice

1 cup dry red wine

2 to 3 cups cubed carrots or turnips

ORANGE GREMOLATA

½ cup minced Italian parsley

6 tablespoons freshly grated Parmesan cheese

¼ cup minced orange peel

4 large cloves garlic

1. Preheat the oven to 350°F (180°C). Trim all exterior fat from the ribs. Generously salt and pepper the meat using about 2 teaspoons salt and 2 teaspoons black pepper total. Combine the flour and fennel seeds in a shallow bowl. Dredge the short ribs in the flour mixture.

2. Heat ¼ cup of the olive oil in a large roasting pan over medium-high heat and brown the short ribs, in batches, on all sides. Remove to a plate.

3. Add additional oil as necessary and cook the onions in the same pan until softened, 3 to 4 minutes. Add the garlic and mushrooms. Sauté until the mushrooms are colored, about 4 minutes; stir frequently to avoid sticking. Add the ingredients through the red wine. Stir well to get any browned bits off the bottom of the pan.

4. Bring to a simmer; add back the browned short ribs, bone sides up. Press the short ribs down to submerge in the sauce as much as possible. Cover tightly with aluminum foil and bake 2 hours, until the meat is fork-tender, turning after 1 hour.

5. At the end of 2 hours turn the short ribs over again and add the carrots, pushing them under the sauce. Cover the pan again and cook for 25 to 30 minutes, until the carrots are soft and the meat is very tender. Remove the roasting pan from the oven and spoon off any grease from the surface of the sauce. Discard bay leaves.

   (The dish can be prepared through Step 5 up to two days in advance and refrigerated. This chilling provides the advantage of allowing you to easily remove any excess grease from the pan. Reheat gently, covered.)

6. **TO MAKE THE GREMOLATA:** Grind the ingredients to a paste in a spice grinder or mini food processor. Serve the short ribs with the pan sauce and vegetables and a generous sprinkling of the gremolata.

▓ VARIATIONS

Cuban-Flavored Braised Beef Short Ribs Most of the changes in this recipe take place in Step 3. Replace the tomato paste with ½ cup seedless raisins or dried cherries. Increase the orange juice to a total of ½ cup. Replace ½ cup of the red wine with ½ cup fresh lime juice. Replace the bay leaves with ¼ teaspoon ground allspice. Add ¾ cup pitted green Spanish olives, ⅓ cup drained capers and 1 seeded, minced jalapeño chile.

The gremolata can be given a Caribbean flair by replacing the orange zest with ¼ cup minced lime zest (which you removed from the limes before using for juice) and replacing the parsley with ½ cup chopped cilantro.

Five Sea Creature Stew (Cioppino)

Cioppino, like cassoulet, always elicits sighs of longing from my friends. It is the kind of dish that one orders in a good seafood restaurant because it is too hard to make at home. Wrong! The following recipe simplifies the concept, breaking it down into mostly done-ahead steps. As long as you have excellent seafood, it is a manageable centerpiece for a casual feast.

Cioppino was originally a simple stew based on what a fisherman caught that day. Let yourself go when shopping for this dish; buy what looks good and fresh, aiming for a combination of four to five types of fish and shellfish. Some cooks put a giant garlic crouton in the bottom of each bowl before adding the soup. At the very least, serve lots of crisped garlic bread on the side.

Casual • Pricey • Healthy

PARTY TIME PREPARATIONS: About 12 minutes of attended cooking to serve.

SERVING EQUIPMENT: A large tureen (you could even use the cooking kettle for a really casual party), serving spoon or ladle and large soup bowls for the guests.

BEVERAGE TO ACCOMPANY: Barbera, Pinot Grigio, Sancerre, Chianti

Makes 8 to 10 servings

18 small clams, scrubbed and rinsed well	¼ cup finely shredded fresh basil
18 green-lipped mussels, scrubbed and debearded	1 tablespoon fresh thyme
1 (750-ml) bottle dry white wine	1½ tablespoons minced fresh oregano
1 cup chopped fresh Italian parsley	¼ teaspoon fennel seeds
¼ cup olive oil	1 teaspoon kosher salt and freshly ground black pepper
1 large onion, minced	2 pounds white fish fillets, cut in large chunks (sea bass, cod, rock cod, halibut; albacore is also excellent)
¾ cup diced scallions (white and green parts)	
1 cup diced red bell pepper	½ pound lump crabmeat or lobster meat chunks or 2 freshly cooked whole Dungeness crabs, cleaned and roughly chopped
2 tablespoons minced garlic	
¼ cup tomato paste	¾ pound medium shrimp, butterflied with shell and tail left on
½ teaspoon red chile flakes	
2 bay leaves	4 lemons, quartered
2½ cups canned crushed tomatoes, including juice	

1. Put the clams and mussels in a saucepan with 1 cup of the wine and ¼ cup of the parsley. Cover, bring to a boil and steam until they are cooked and open, 5 to 6 min-

utes. Discard any that remain closed. Let cool; strain the liquid through a cheese-cloth and reserve. Cover the shellfish and set aside.

2. Heat the olive oil in a large (6-quart or larger) kettle over medium heat. Add the onion, scallions and bell pepper and sauté about 5 minutes, until the onion is softened. Add the garlic and sauté 2 to 3 minutes.

3. Add the tomato paste, chile flakes, bay leaves, tomatoes, basil, thyme, oregano, fennel seeds, ½ cup of the parsley, the reserved liquid from the clams and mussels, 1 teaspoon salt and several grindings of black pepper. Simmer uncovered 5 minutes. Add remaining wine and simmer uncovered 25 minutes longer to develop the flavors. (The dish can be prepared through this step up to 1 day in advance and refrigerated. If refrigerated, bring the sauce back to a gentle simmer and continue with directions.)

4. Add the white fish chunks to the pot and simmer gently for 5 minutes. Add the crabmeat and shrimp, submerging them in the broth. Cook for 3 to 4 minutes, until the shrimp are pink and firm. Taste for salt and pepper. Add the clams and mussels and ladle broth over them to heat through, being careful not to break up the crab chunks. Remove from the heat, cover and let sit for 3 to 4 minutes before serving.

5. **TO SERVE:** Ladle the assorted seafood into each bowl, cover with broth and sprinkle generously with remaining ¼ cup parsley. Each bowl should be served with lemon wedges.

▒ VARIATION

New England–Style Cioppino with Spicy Sausage Add 8 to 10 ounces fully cooked spicy sausage, sliced into discs, at the same time as the fish in Step 4. (I particularly like Aidell's Chicken Habanero sausage.) Because the sausage is spicy, delete the red chile flakes. If you use an Italian-style sausage, you may wish to delete the fennel seeds as well because they are frequently added to Italian sausages.

CURRY ABCS

This curry was like a performance of Beethoven's Ninth Symphony that I'd once heard . . . especially the last movement, with everything screaming and banging "Joy." It stunned, it made one fear great art. My father could say nothing after the meal.

—Anthony Burgess

Curry means many things to many people. The word itself describes both a sauce and a blend of dry spices. Also, some cooks introduce their curry blend to a recipe in its dry-roasted form, while others make a wet paste by adding water. In Japan, curry is sold in blocks, made of curry spices, animal fats and fruit paste. In the Far East, where the spicing originated, each cook customarily mixes her own blend. You can buy a versatile Madras-style curry blend at most local grocery stores. My favorite is Sun brand in the metallic canister. Other places to find premixed curry blends—and there are a nearly infinite number from which to choose—include local independent spice stores and mail-order sources. I have included a recipe below with classic spices if you would like to make your own, inspired by curry divas Julie Sahni and Madhur Jaffrey.

2 tablespoons coriander seed	5 whole cloves garlic
1 tablespoon ground cumin	1 tablespoon red chile flakes
2 teaspoons freshly ground black pepper	1 teaspoon kosher salt
2 teaspoons brown mustard seed	1½ teaspoons turmeric
1 teaspoon fenugreek seed	

Blend spices. Grind to a fine powder at time of use (you can use an old handheld coffee grinder for this task).

VARIATION
Add 4 teaspoons paprika and 1 teaspoon cayenne pepper for red curry.

Shrimp Curry in Coconut-Tomato Broth

Curry is an ideal dish for entertaining. It improves with long, slow cooking and making ahead of time, guests get to participate by building their own dish with the varied condiments, and its brilliant colors and exotic flavors seem festive any time of year. When I tell guests that curry is on the menu, the response is always a groaning yum. The shrimp curry is also excellent with a pound or two of scrubbed green-lipped mussels added into the sauce to cook with the shrimp. When I add the mussels I use fewer shrimp.

Buffet • Completed in Advance

PARTY TIME PREPARATIONS: Can be prepared up to the night before and then reheated after guests arrive.

SERVING EQUIPMENT: To serve family style you'll need a large platter or bowl for the rice and for the curry, 4 to 5 small bowls for condiments, 2 large serving spoons and 4 to 5 small ones.

BEVERAGE TO ACCOMPANY: Beer, spicy tea, spicy dry white wine like Alsatian Gewürztraminer or Viognier

Makes 8 servings

2 heaping tablespoons chopped garlic (about 8 cloves)

1½ tablespoons chopped fresh ginger

4 red Thai chiles or 2 serrano chiles, seeded and chopped

¾ cup water

¼ cup peanut or vegetable oil

2-inch stick of cinnamon, roughly crushed

2 bay leaves

2½ cups minced onions

2 to 3 tablespoons curry powder, preferably Sun brand

½ teaspoon ground cardamom

1½ cups minced, canned Roma tomatoes

2 tablespoons chopped fresh cilantro

1 cup coconut milk

2 teaspoons kosher salt, or to taste

¾ cup plain low-fat or full-fat yogurt

3 pounds large (16 to a pound or larger) shrimp, peeled and deveined, tail on

2 tablespoons fresh lime or lemon juice

1 teaspoon garam masala

½ cup of each of four or more of these essential condiments: shredded unsweetened coconut, chopped roasted peanuts, raisins, chutney, mango pickle, chopped cilantro, chopped scallions, toasted pumpkin seeds, poppy seeds, fried shallots

1. Combine the garlic, ginger, chiles and 2 tablespoons of the water in a blender and puree.

2. Heat the oil over medium-high heat in a 14-inch sauté pan or Dutch oven. When hot, add the cinnamon stick and bay leaves and sauté for 5 seconds. Add the onions and sauté until golden brown, 7 to 10 minutes. Add the ginger mixture and sauté until aromatic and the water has evaporated. (This develops the flavor.)

3. Stir in the curry powder and ground cardamom plus 1 to 2 additional tablespoons of water. Sauté for 1 to 2 minutes, until aromatic. Add the tomatoes, cilantro, remaining water, coconut milk and salt. Stir to blend, then whisk in the yogurt. Lower the heat and simmer for 5 to 7 minutes to thicken.

4. Add the shrimp and bring the mixture to a boil. Reduce the heat, cover and simmer for 10 to 12 minutes, until the shrimp are cooked and the sauce has thickened.

5. Remove the curry from the heat. Stir in the lime juice and taste for additional salt. Sprinkle in the garam masala. Let the dish rest for at least 5 minutes before serving. (This can be prepared the day before serving, cooled to room temperature, then refrigerated. Reheat over low heat.)

6. **TO SERVE:** On either a flat platter or individual dinner plates, spoon the curry over a mound of basmati or jasmine rice. On the side, offer at least four of the condiments listed above in small bowls for guests to serve themselves.

✹ VARIATIONS

Lamb Curry Replace the shrimp with 3 pounds boneless shoulder or leg of lamb cut into 2 × 1-inch chunks. Toss the lamb thoroughly with an additional ¾ cup yogurt, salt, pepper and 2 tablespoons minced ginger. Marinate for 2 hours at room temperature or for 12 hours in the refrigerator.

Wipe the lamb chunks dry and sauté in a skillet over medium-high heat in 2 to 3 tablespoons of vegetable oil until browned on all sides. Prepare the sauce as for shrimp in Steps 1 to 3. Add the browned pieces of lamb to the sauce and stir to coat with the sauce. Reduce the heat to a gentle simmer and cover. Cook, stirring occasionally, for 1 hour and 15 minutes to 2 hours, until the lamb is fork-tender. You may need to add 1 to 2 tablespoons more liquid toward the end of the cooking.

Remove from the heat. Skim off any excess fat. Stir in the lime juice and taste for additional salt. Sprinkle in the garam masala. Let rest for at least 5 minutes before serving.

Chicken Curry Replace the shrimp with 3 pounds of boneless, skinless chicken breasts and thighs cut into 2-inch chunks. Dredge the chicken in ⅓ cup flour mixed with salt and pepper. Shake off any excess. In a large sauté or roasting pan, heat 3 tablespoons vegetable oil over medium-high heat, add the pieces of chicken and turn to brown quickly on all sides. Do not overcrowd the pan. Remove the browned chicken from the pan to a plate.

Use the same pan to prepare the sauce, as for the shrimp in Steps 1 to 3. Add the browned pieces of chicken in place of shrimp, and stir to coat. Reduce the heat to a gentle simmer and cover. Cook, stirring occasionally, for 25 to 35 minutes, until the chicken is fork-tender. You may need to add 1 to 2 tablespoons more liquid toward the end of the cooking.

Remove from the heat. Skim off any excess oil. Stir in lime juice and taste for additional salt. Sprinkle in the garam masala. Let rest for at least 5 minutes before serving.

WINE PAIRINGS FOR SPICY AND ASIAN FOODS

Spicy foods—those relying on exotic seasonings and/or heat from chiles—present interesting wine-pairing challenges that call for a bit more creativity than usual, which is why when they work, the effect can be astonishing. Most wines pair reasonably well with the savory, European-type cuisines alongside of which they developed, but Asian, Hispanic, Caribbean and African cuisines arose without corresponding wine cultures, and beer often seems like the safest beverage to serve. There are a lot of wines that will match these dishes beautifully, though. I rely on wines, mostly whites, with lots of bright acidity and fresh fruit flavors, like dry Riesling, Chenin Blanc, Alsatian Pinot Blanc and Viognier, to stand up to assertive spicy flavors. The key is in the fruitiness, which doesn't necessarily mean sweetness, though that can help, especially when the dish is *really* hot. Even a classic beef dish like Thai panang neau tastes great with a crisp and cold, fruity white wine. As for reds, I've had great luck with young Zinfandels, fruity Merlots and cool Gamays with dishes like chili con carne or rogan josh, my favorite Indian red lamb curry with plenty of heat.

Quintessential Herb Roasted Chicken

Bringing a whole roast chicken to your dinner table conjures warm holiday memories without the all-day fuss of cooking a turkey. Roast chicken is one of America's classic comfort foods, right up there with its cousin, chicken soup. However, it can also be the welcome centerpiece for an elegant supper. This quintessential chicken is crispy, moist and fragrant. The addition of shiitake mushrooms makes the recipe a little more formal. The final variation, even simpler to prepare, uses the Tahini-Lemon Vinaigrette (page 134) to marinate and create a sauce for the chicken all in one step. Garnished with pomegranate seeds and/or cilantro, this variation is a great twist on a classic and makes a beautiful presentation.

Casual • Formal • Quick and Easy

PARTY TIME PREPARATIONS: Can be prepared the night before and baked after guests arrive.

SERVING EQUIPMENT: Serving platter and carving utensils.

BEVERAGE TO ACCOMPANY: Gewürztraminer, Riesling, Viognier

Makes 8 servings

CHICKEN

¼ cup fresh lemon juice

2 (4- to 5-pound) whole roasting chickens, preferably kosher or organic

1½ tablespoons Dijon mustard

4 tablespoons unsalted butter, softened

2 tablespoons mashed garlic

¾ teaspoon kosher salt

2 tablespoons minced fresh thyme or tarragon

4 fresh thyme sprigs, plus additional for garnish

1 lemon, sliced

⅓ cup chicken broth

VERMOUTH-MUSTARD SAUCE

⅔ cup chicken broth

⅔ cup vermouth

1 teaspoon Dijon mustard

¼ cup whipping cream (optional)

2 to 3 tablespoons chopped fresh tarragon or parsley

1. Drizzle the lemon juice all over the chickens and rub it in.
2. Mix together the mustard, 1 tablespoon of the butter, the garlic, salt and thyme. Gently loosen the skin on the chickens over the breast and leg meat. Rub some of the butter mixture evenly on the flesh. Pull the skin back into place and rub the remaining butter mixture all over the outsides of the chickens. Generously salt and

pepper the cavities and the outsides of the chickens. Put 2 thyme sprigs and some lemon slices into the cavity of each chicken. Tie the drumsticks together with kitchen twine. Cover the chicken with plastic and let marinate in the refrigerator for 6 to 8 hours or ½ hour at room temperature.

3. Preheat the oven to 425°F (220°C). Select a shallow, metal roasting pan and roasting rack large enough for both chickens. Rub the chickens with the remaining butter. Place the chickens, breast side up, on the roasting rack and roast for 20 minutes.

4. Lower the heat to 350°F (180°C). Roast 10 minutes; add the broth to the pan. Roast another 45 to 65 minutes, basting several times with pan juices. Chicken is done when the thigh juices run clear when pierced and an instant-read thermometer inserted in the thigh registers 170°F (75°C).

5. Remove the pan from the oven, tip the chickens to empty their cooking juices into the pan and transfer the chickens to a large bowl, tails down. Tent the chickens with foil.

6. **TO MAKE THE SAUCE:** Spoon off any excess fat from the roasting pan and place the pan over medium-high heat. When the juices in the pan are sizzling, add the vermouth and stir to dislodge the browned bits. When this is all mixed together, add the mustard and cooking juices that drained from the chicken into the bowl. Stir in the cream, if using. Simmer 7 to 10 minutes to thicken and blend. Add the tarragon and season with salt and pepper to taste.

7. Cut the chickens into quarters and serve with the sauce and a sprig of thyme.

VARIATIONS

Roast Chicken with Shiitake Mushrooms Toss 24 cleaned, stems removed, shiitake mushrooms (about ½ pound) and 2 medium onions, quartered lengthwise, with 2 tablespoons olive oil to coat. When you lower the temperature in Step 4, add the mushrooms, onions and ⅓ cup stock to the pan. Tuck the vegetables under and around the chicken. They may need to be turned when you baste the chicken.

Remove the vegetables from the pan along with the chicken in Step 5. Cut the mushrooms in half and add into the sauce along with the broth in Step 6. Serve the onions with the chicken and sauce.

Roast Chicken with Tahini Replace the butter mixture in Step 2 with Tahini-Lemon Vinaigrette (page 134), but omit the red bell pepper. In Step 3, do not rub the chickens with butter. Brush the surface of the chickens with 2 tablespoons olive oil after they have been in the oven for 10 minutes. The chickens may need to be tented with foil if they become too dark before the meat is done.

Do not make the sauce. Combine the pan juices from the roasting pan and the bowl where the chicken rested before carving for a sauce.

Serve garnished with ½ cup pomegranate seeds and ½ cup chopped cilantro.

ORGANIC CHICKEN

Organic chicken is my bird of choice. Organically raised chickens are allowed to mature naturally without feeding on chemicals or growth hormones. As a result, these are the most flavorful, fresh-tasting chickens for sale. They aren't yet available in every grocery. However, as consumers become aware of their superior quality, I believe they will become more widely available throughout the country. These chemical-free chickens are worth looking for. As of October 2002, the government issued certified organic labels to qualified growers. On the other hand, the term free-range may or may not indicate a naturally raised chicken; the labeling is ill-defined and mostly unregulated.

Easy as "Chicken Pot Pie"

This simple and impressive dish can be prepared up to a week in advance, frozen and popped in the oven at party time. I serve it on a plate by itself with a garnish of fresh herbs and a drizzle of pesto, or marooned in a pool of couscous to soak up the glorious juices. You don't really need any vegetable sides since they're all in the "bag." Purchased puff pastry provides the crispy, easy, buttery crust.

    This can also be prepared in individual oven-to-table bowls or as a large pie in a 13 × 9-inch baking dish.

Casual • Completed in Advance

PARTY TIME PREPARATIONS: **Bake and serve.**

SERVING EQUIPMENT: **If on a buffet, platter and large spatula.**

BEVERAGE TO ACCOMPANY: **Côte de Rhône, Gamay Beaujolais, Pouilly-Fuissé**

Makes 6 (1½-cup) or 8 (1-cup) portions (10 cups of filling)

1½ cups chicken broth (if canned, use low-sodium)

2½ ounces dried porcini or shiitake mushrooms

2 pounds boneless, skinless chicken breasts

2 cups julienne carrots

1½ cups frozen, thawed pearl onions

1½ cups halved sugar snap peas or lima beans

6 tablespoons unsalted butter

½ cup minced shallots (about 6)

1½ tablespoons minced garlic

5 tablespoons all-purpose flour

¾ cup dry vermouth

2 teaspoons grated lemon zest

2 tablespoons minced fresh thyme or tarragon

½ cup minced fresh Italian parsley

Dash hot pepper sauce or sprinkle of cayenne pepper

1 teaspoon each kosher salt and white pepper

4 slices bacon, cooked, crumbled (optional)

4 (17-ounce) packages frozen puff pastry, thawed in the refrigerator

1. Heat ⅓ cup of the chicken broth until very hot. Cover dried mushrooms with the hot chicken broth; set aside to soak until cool. Drain the mushrooms and reserve the liquid. Cut any large mushrooms in half.

2. Cut the chicken breasts into 2-inch chunks. In a large microwave-safe container combine the chicken and ½ cup of the chicken broth. Cover loosely and cook on High for 3 minutes. Add the carrots, pearl onions and sugar snap peas. Re-cover and cook on High for 4 to 5 minutes, until the chicken is firm and barely cooked. Drain and reserve the liquid.

3. Add the mushroom broth and the chicken poaching liquid to remaining chicken broth. Heat the mixture in the microwave or on the stovetop to hot but not boiling, and remove from heat.

4. Melt the butter in a large saucepan over medium heat. Add the shallots and garlic and sauté for 2 to 3 minutes, until softened. Add the flour, whisking to blend. Cook, stirring, 2 to 3 minutes. Whisk in the hot broth mixture and vermouth. Simmer briskly, stirring until thick, 5 to 6 minutes. Let cool.

5. In a large bowl, combine all the vegetables, chicken, lemon zest and herbs.

6. Add the sauce to the bowl of chicken and vegetables and toss to combine. Add the hot pepper sauce, salt and white pepper. Stir in bacon, if using.

7. On a lightly floured board, roll out the puff pastry sheets to about 13 inches each. For each individual pot pie, cut 2 pieces of pastry from each sheet of pastry; 1 6-inch circle and 1 7-inch circle. Mound 1 to 1½ cups filling on the 6-inch piece. Brush the edge with cold water. Drape the 7-inch piece over the chicken and press onto the bottom circle. Roll the bottom edge over the top to form a ropelike border. Using the tines of a fork, roll up and over the rope, pressing firmly to adhere. Chill for at least 30 minutes or freeze up to 1 week in advance. (If you have small oven-proof bowls, you could fill them with the same amount of filling, brush the edge of the bowl with cold water and top with a circle of pastry.)

8. Preheat the oven to 425°F (220°C). Transfer the pot pies to a baking sheet lined with parchment paper and a dusting of cornmeal. Bake for 30 minutes, until golden (if you are cooking in bowls, bake for 20 minutes). Remove and let rest for 5 to 10 minutes before serving.

※ VARIATION

Chicken Pot Pie with Greek Flavors Use a combination of boneless chicken breast and thighs in this heartier-flavored dish. In Step 4, whisk in 3 tablespoons brandy and 1¼ cups grated kasseri with the chicken broth and vermouth and cook until thick.

In Step 6, add ½ cup pitted kalamata olives, 2 tablespoons minced fresh oregano, ¼ teaspoon freshly grated nutmeg and ¼ teaspoon ground cinnamon. Increase the lemon zest to 1 tablespoon. Complete as directed above.

Lamb Shashlik

Kebobs, brochettes, skewers, souvlaki, shashlik—these all mean grilling on a skewer in five different languages, and the method exists in many more. The fact that this kind of cooking appears in so many cuisines reflects the ease with which great, festive meals can be prepared from marinated ingredients threaded on a skewer and cooked over a hot fire.

When serving a kebob entrée, give your guests the opportunity to create their own special dish by providing a selection of garnishes and wraps. In the Middle East, large pita bread is often used to grasp the meat and slide it off the skewer, creating a "sandwich." Another community favors serving the skewers on a bed of rice or couscous. Either style is perfect accompanied by grilled eggplant with the Tahini-Lemon Vinaigrette on page 134. As variations, Greek flavors are used to create a souvlaki-style dish prepared with swordfish, lemons and olives for a light, summery meal. A light vegetarian brochette with fresh mozzarella rounds out the mix.

Quick and Easy • Healthy • Vegetarian Option

PARTY TIME PREPARATIONS: Can be prepared up to the night before and then grilled after guests arrive.

SERVING EQUIPMENT: Large platter, serving fork and spoon or tongs.

BEVERAGE TO ACCOMPANY: Shiraz, Sauvignon Blanc, Pinot Grigio

Makes 8 servings, 16 to 18 skewers

4 pounds boned leg of lamb, trimmed and cut into 1-inch cubes (see note, page 98)	5 yellow or red bell peppers, cut into 2-inch squares
2 bunches green onions (white parts only), cut into 2-inch lengths	1 recipe Red Wine Marinade (page 131)

1. Toss the lamb cubes, onions and bell peppers with the marinade; cover and marinate in the refrigerator for 24 hours or at room temperature for 2 hours. The skewers should be about 12 inches long. If you are using bamboo skewers, soak in water for at least 30 minutes before using.

2. Preheat grill to medium-high heat (375°F, 190°C). Assemble each skewer in this order: onion, lamb, bell pepper, onion, lamb, bell pepper, leaving about 2 inches free at each end. Press all of the elements together.

3. Wipe down the hot grill with an oil-soaked paper towel or cut lemon. Arrange the skewers on the grill. Cook for 10 minutes on the first side. Turn using tongs and brush with the marinade. Cook on the second side for about 10 minutes. At the end

of a total of 20 minutes on the grill, check the lamb for doneness. For medium-rare, the meat should be pink in the center and slightly brown toward the exterior.

(The finished skewers can be held up to half an hour in a 200°F [95°C] oven if well wrapped and drizzled with a little olive oil.)

✸ VARIATIONS

Swordfish Souvlaki Replace the lamb with 2½ to 3 pounds swordfish or ahi tuna fillets cut into 1-inch cubes. Prepare the Greek Marinade (page 132). Toss the fish with the marinade and let marinate for 20 to 30 minutes at room temperature or 1 hour in the refrigerator.

Do not use the green onions and red bell peppers from the lamb recipe. Slice a lemon into paper-thin discs (about 35 slices). Add the lemon slices, 32 (1-inch) cherry tomatoes and 32 pitted kalamata olives to the marinated fish mixture and toss to coat.

Assemble each skewer by piercing a piece of fish, a lemon slice folded in half (skewer through the white pith so that it will stay firmly in place), a cherry tomato and an olive. Repeat with another piece of fish, lemon, tomato and olive, and end with a final piece of fish. Wedge all of the elements tightly together on the skewers.

Prepare the grill and cook as in Step 3, but for only 2 to 3 minutes per side. Fish should just start to flake when done.

Vegetarian Brochette Prepare the Greek Marinade (page 132) with the addition of 1 teaspoon salt. Toss the marinade with 30 (1-inch) cherry tomatoes; 3 red bell peppers, cut into 2-inch squares; 32 white button mushrooms; 1 pound fresh mozzarella, cut into 1 inch cubes, or bocconcini. Let marinate for 3 to 8 hours in the refrigerator. Toss the vegetables with the marinade about every half hour. Select 25 basic leaves.

To prepare the skewers, pierce a mushroom, a leaf of basil, a piece of bell pepper with a piece of mozzarella nestled in the curve (this prevents the cheese from melting too quickly) and a tomato. Repeat once more. Prepare grill as in Step 3, but adjust the temperature to medium. Cook skewers, turning occasionally, for 12 to 14 minutes, until the bell peppers have softened and the vegetables are colored.

NOTE: On average, a 7- to 8-pound bone-in leg of lamb will yield 5 pounds when boned, and about 4 pounds when cleaned of excess fat and tissue.

Chicken Provençal

Chicken Provençal is so simple to prepare and so delicious that it is one of the dishes I serve most often to company. This is essentially a two-step recipe: marinate and bake. The Chicken Ali Bab variation is an exotic blend of sweet, sour and salty that I find addictive. Both recipes create such luscious juices while cooking that it's a crime to serve them without jasmine rice or couscous to soak up the flavors. This is outstanding followed by a dessert of cheese, dates and almonds.

Buffet • Quick and Easy • Inexpensive

PARTY TIME PREPARATIONS: Bake and serve.

SERVING EQUIPMENT: Large, deep platter or shallow bowl and serving spoon.

BEVERAGE TO ACCOMPANY: Spanish red wine such as Temparnillo or Zinfandel

Makes 6 to 8 servings

6 pounds chicken thighs or combined breasts and thighs, trimmed of all excess skin and fat

2 tablespoons dried thyme

1½ tablespoons ground rosemary

1½ teaspoons kosher salt

3 tablespoons minced garlic

⅓ cup chopped oil-packed sun-dried tomatoes

½ teaspoon freshly ground coarse black pepper

¼ cup olive oil

1½ cups sliced mushrooms

2 teaspoons sugar

3 tablespoons white wine vinegar or fresh lemon juice

½ cup pitted kalamata olives

⅓ cup capers, drained

½ cup white wine or dry vermouth

½ cup fine bread crumbs mixed with ½ cup freshly grated Parmesan cheese

1. Combine all of the ingredients from chicken through capers in a large bowl and toss to blend well. Transfer to a large, resealable plastic bag. (I usually put that into another bag before refrigerating to catch any leaks.) Refrigerate overnight or for at least 12 hours.

2. Preheat the oven to 350°F (180°C). Pour the contents of the plastic bag into a large, flat baking dish (preferably Le Creuset). Arrange the chicken, bone side down, in one layer. Pour the white wine over the chicken and bake for 20 minutes. Sprinkle the crumb mixture evenly over the chicken and put back in the oven to bake for 30 to 35 minutes, until browned and the chicken is cooked. Baste two or three times with the pan juices.

3. **TO SERVE:** Spoon the pan juices and seasonings over the chicken.

Chicken Ali Bab Make substitutions as follows in Step 1. Any ingredient not mentioned is left in the recipe. Replace the thyme with 2 tablespoons ground coriander, replace the rosemary with 2½ tablespoons ground cumin, replace the sun-dried tomatoes with 1 lemon, sliced very thin (in addition to the lemon juice called for in the above recipe), replace the mushrooms with 16 shallots, peeled and halved. Omit the olives. Add ⅔ cup dried apricots or prunes and ¾ teaspoon cinnamon. Combine and marinate as directed above.

In Step 2, instead of bread crumbs and Parmesan cheese, top the chicken with ⅔ cup packed light brown sugar sprinkled over the chicken when you first put it in the oven. Proceed with the directions above. Cilantro is great as an alternative to the parsley.

Strata Vermont

This delicate, low-stress relative of the soufflé is beautiful when it's served, as the golden custard and filling layers reveal themselves. Classic Vermont ingredients are the focus in the first recipe, combining maple syrup, Vermont white Cheddar and crispy green apples. It is excellent for a brunch or luncheon buffet. The first variation offers robust Italian flavors. The Shiitake Mushroom and Brie Strata is a sophisticated vegetarian entrée.

Buffet • Completed in Advance • Vegetarian Option

PARTY TIME PREPARATIONS: Can be prepared the night before and baked after guests arrive.

SERVING EQUIPMENT: To serve from a buffet, an attractive baking dish (this can't be transferred), and 2 large serving spoons.

BEVERAGE TO ACCOMPANY: Barbera, Rioja, Beaujolais

Makes 6 to 8 brunch servings

1 loaf challah or egg bread	¼ teaspoon freshly grated nutmeg
½ pound thick-cut bacon, or 6 ounces pancetta, chopped into large chunks	Pinch cayenne pepper
¾ cup chopped onion	1 teaspoon white pepper
4 cups thinly sliced, halved crosswise tart apples (Granny Smith)	8 ounces chèvre
1 tablespoon maple syrup	4 cups grated Vermont white Cheddar (about 1 pound)
5 eggs	¼ cup chopped fresh thyme or basil or 3 tablespoons minced rosemary
1 egg yolk	¼ cup chopped fresh chives
1¾ cups milk	¼ cup freshly grated Parmesan
2 cups heavy cream	
1 teaspoon salt	

1. Butter a 3- to 3½-quart casserole. Cut the bread into enough ¾-inch-thick slices to form 2 layers in your casserole; toast lightly in the oven or toaster, and set aside.

2. In a sauté pan, cook the bacon over low heat for 3 to 5 minutes, until the meat is cooked through but not crisp. Add the onion, apples and maple syrup and sauté 5 minutes, until the onion softens. Remove from heat, drain off the fat and set aside.

3. In a large bowl combine the eggs, egg yolk, milk, cream, salt, nutmeg, cayenne and white pepper. Set aside.

4. Cover the bottom of the casserole with one layer of the toasted bread. Evenly cover with half of the chèvre, Cheddar, apple mixture and herbs. Cover with the remain-

ing slices of bread, remaining Cheddar, apple mixture, chèvre and herbs. Sprinkle with the Parmesan cheese. Pour the egg mixture to within 1 inch of the top of the dish (depending on your pan shape, there may be extra liquid). Let the dish rest, covered and lightly weighted, for 3 hours or overnight in the refrigerator.

5. Preheat the oven to 350°F (180°C). Bake the dish uncovered for 35 to 40 minutes, until bubbling, puffed slightly and set (a knife inserted in the middle will come out clean). Remove from the oven and let rest at least 10 minutes before serving.

✹ VARIATIONS

Italian Essentials Strata Replace the apples and maple syrup with 1½ cups finely sliced red or yellow bell pepper. Replace the assertive Cheddar with mellower Fontina or Taleggio cheese. Use basil instead of thyme. This is excellent with the addition of ½ cup chopped sun-dried tomatoes and a pureed head of roasted garlic whipped into the egg mixture. Complete as above.

Shiitake Mushroom and Brie Strata For a luscious vegetarian variation, do not use the pancetta, apple and maple syrup. In Step 2, heat 4 tablespoons olive oil in the sauté pan; add ½ pound thinly sliced shiitake mushrooms and sauté for 2 to 3 minutes, until soft. Add 1½ cups finely sliced fennel bulb and the ¾ cup chopped onion and sauté until brown. You may need to add up to ¼ cup white wine to keep the mushrooms from sticking to the pan. Replace the Cheddar with 1 pound of Brie, cut into chunks. Thyme would be the better herb choice to enhance the woodsy flavor of the mushrooms. Complete as above.

Mole Poblano–Style Chili with Beans

The discovery of a new dish does more for the happiness of the human race than the discovery of a star.

—Jean Anthelme Brillat-Savarin

For years when friends urged me to try mole poblano, a chocolate and chile sauce from Puebla, Mexico, I shuddered. And then I tasted my friend Christopher's elegant sauce. I was hooked. This chili recipe is the result of that ensuing infatuation with mole's complex, earthy flavors. I've infused a hearty Southwestern chili con carne with some of the exotic tastes of a traditional mole. I find that guests are seduced by the taste of this chili while remaining mystified as to all of the ingredients. It's fun to reveal that my secret is chocolate. Like most chili, this is better if made a day or two in advance and gently reheated.

Casual • Buffet • Completed in Advance

PARTY TIME PREPARATIONS: Heat and serve.

SERVING EQUIPMENT: Soup tureen; spackle ware, Dutch oven or terra-cotta casserole; large ladle; and small bowls and spoons for garnishes.

BEVERAGE TO ACCOMPANY: Beer, margaritas

Makes 6 to 8 servings

CHILI

2 large dried ancho chiles (see note, below)

2 dried pasilla chiles (see note, below)

1 to 2 tablespoons minced chipotle chile in adobo

½ cup raisins

2½ cups beef broth or Mexican beer

4 tablespoons olive or vegetable oil

3 pounds boneless pork picnic shoulder roast, cut into 1-inch cubes and seasoned with salt and pepper

3 large yellow onions, diced

1 teaspoon kosher salt

8 cloves garlic, minced

1 tablespoon ground cumin

2 tablespoons chile powder

½ teaspoon ground cinnamon

1½ teaspoons dried thyme

1 tablespoon dried Mexican oregano

2 ounces unsweetened chocolate, roughly chopped

1 cup canned crushed tomatoes

2 or 3 (15-ounce) cans black or pinto beans, drained

2 tablespoons yellow cornmeal or ground almonds

TO SERVE

1 cup sour cream or *crema fresca* (similar to mild sour cream)

¼ cup fresh orange juice

2 tablespoons grated orange zest

¼ cup toasted sesame seeds

½ cup chopped fresh cilantro

1. Put the ancho and pasilla chiles in a microwave-safe bowl. Cover with water and heat on High for 2 minutes (or cover with boiling water). Let stand 20 minutes or until very soft. Remove the seeds and stems and reserve the soaking liquid.

2. Put the soaked chiles in a blender along with the chipotle chiles, raisins, ¼ cup of the soaking liquid and ¼ cup of the beef broth. Puree until smooth.

3. Heat 2 tablespoons of the oil in a large, Dutch oven over medium-high heat. Add the pork cubes in batches and sauté, turning to brown all sides. Remove to a bowl as they are done, adding more oil as necessary.

4. Add the onions, salt and garlic to the same pan and sauté until the onions are tender and golden, about 8 minutes. Add all of the spices and herbs and sauté until fragrant, about 3 minutes. Add the chile puree, reduce the heat and simmer about 5 minutes, stirring frequently. It will become quite thick; add a little broth if necessary. Add the chocolate and stir until melted.

5. Return the browned meat to the pan along with the remaining broth and tomatoes. Reduce the heat to low, cover and simmer for 1½ hours or until the meat is fork-tender.

6. Add the drained beans. Taste for seasoning and add salt, pepper or more chipotle chile as desired. Stir in the cornmeal if you want to thicken the texture. Simmer until the beans are heated through and the chili is the desired thickness. (The chili can be made and refrigerated up to 2 days before serving.)

7. **TO SERVE:** Combine the sour cream, orange juice and zest. Serve a dollop on each individual bowl of chili. Top with a sprinkling of sesame seeds and chopped cilantro.

✺ VARIATIONS

Beef Chili Replace the pork with 3 pounds beef brisket or chuck roast and proceed as directed.

Chili Con Carne If you don't want beans in your chili, omit the beans, reduce the beef broth by ½ cup and serve the finished dish over rice or posole.

NOTE: Ancho chile is the dried form of the mild poblano. It has a sweet, earthy flavor. Pasilla chile is the dried form of the chilaca chile. It is fairly hot and adds a subtle flavor to sauces. It is also called chile negro.

THE RIESLING POLEMIC

A lot of people say they don't like Riesling, believing that it is sweet and therefore icky. However, my suspicion is that they only *think* they don't like Riesling. There have always been world-class Rieslings and now wine drinkers everywhere are waking up to them.

Riesling's greatest asset is its ability to complement many different cuisines. Americans enjoy an incredible array of food styles; we'll have sushi one night, Tex-Mex the next, Thai, Tuscan, Chinese or French, French, Vietnamese, or Bolivian, or Spanish the next. The list goes on, and it's amazing that you can find a Riesling to accompany the overwhelming majority of them. No other wine can do that.

The key is balance. Sweet or dry, good Rieslings have keenly focused stone fruit flavors offset by bright, clean acidity. Naturally, Rieslings match well with fare from their home turf, like German sauerbraten or Alsatian choucroute, but they are also great with cuisines like American Southwest, Chinese, Thai or Indian. Seafood? No problem. Salads? A natural fit. Even grilled steaks taste great with a rich, dry Riesling. My recommendation: Start experimenting. You'll be amazed.

—Peter Schmalzer

Cedar-Planked Salmon

Smoke-cooking on a plank of cedar is a Native American technique from the Pacific North-west that adapts beautifully to modern tastes. The wood imbues the salmon with a smoky flavor while keeping it tender and moist. I was attracted to this preparation for entertaining because it is simple, dramatic and delicious. Bring the whole, bronzed salmon on a plank to the buffet or dining table to guaranteed oohs from your guests, and that's before they fork into the tender, juicy flesh. This is excellent with the Mashed Potatoes Pommery (page 64).

The maple glaze is a classic complement to the sweet, meaty salmon. This technique can be used on the barbecue or in the oven with equal success on any firm-fleshed fish like swordfish or striped bass as long as the fillets are at least ¾ inch thick.

You will need an untreated Western red cedar plank that is about 6 x 18 inches. These are available at cookware stores or building supply houses.

Quick and Easy • Casual • Formal

PARTY TIME PREPARATIONS: Can be prepared the night before and baked after guests arrive.

SERVING EQUIPMENT: Serving platter and carving utensils.

BEVERAGE TO ACCOMPANY: Cabernet Franc, Sangiovese

Makes 8 servings

MAPLE MARINADE
1 cup pure maple syrup
2 tablespoons minced fresh ginger
¼ cup fresh lemon or lime juice
¼ cup soy sauce
2 tablespoons dry sherry
2 teaspoons minced garlic

SALMON
2 tablespoons vegetable oil
1 (3½-pound) center-cut salmon fillet with skin
1 cup chopped green onions or shaved fennel

1. **TO MAKE THE MARINADE:** Combine all the ingredients in a saucepan. Boil over medium-high heat until reduced to about 1 cup. This can be prepared up to 2 days in advance.

2. Brush half of the marinade on the flesh side of the salmon and let rest at room temperature for 30 minutes.

3. Preheat the oven to 350°F (180°C). Soak the plank in cold water for at least 30 minutes. Sprinkle the plank with the green onions and lay the salmon, skin side down, on top. Brush the salmon once more with the marinade. Roast for 30 to 35

minutes, until firm and opaque and an instant-read thermometer registers about 140°F (60°C).

4. Let the salmon rest for 5 minutes before slicing. Bring remaining marinade to a boil and serve on the side.

🔥 VARIATIONS

Swordfish with Sherry Vinaigrette Substitute Sherry Vinaigrette (page 133) for the Maple Marinade and swordfish for the salmon. Complete as above.

Bass with Greek Marinade Substitute ½ recipe Greek Marinade (page 132) for the Maple Marinade and striped bass for the salmon. Complete as above.

NOTE: To prepare on the barbecue, place the plank over indirect heat, close the lid and cook for about 30 minutes.

New England Clam Chowder with Bacon

Chowder breathes reassurance. It steams consolation.

—Clementine Paddleford

I have always loved the briny succulence of fresh clams and oysters bobbing, barely cooked, in a bath of sweet cream. Absolutely fresh chowder strikes a note of universal appeal; it is simply elegant, evoking a cozy fantasy of sitting by a fire listening to the ocean crash. I serve chowder, in any of the incarnations below, as a first course for a hearty winter dinner or as an anytime entrée for a casual party. It can be mostly prepared in advance with just the last-minute simmering of the mollusks at party time.

The smoked fish variation is a very elegant option suggested by my editor, Jeanette Egan. All of the chowders benefit from the addition of a dollop of nutmeg-scented whipped cream when served.

Casual • Buffet

PARTY TIME PREPARATIONS: Add mollusks and garnish.

SERVING EQUIPMENT: 3-quart soup tureen, ladle and soup bowls.

BEVERAGE TO ACCOMPANY: Chardonnay, Riesling, Viognier

Makes about 12 cups (8 to 10 servings)

½ pound thick-cut bacon, minced (about 6 slices)

2 cups minced onions

1 tablespoon minced garlic

1½ cups thinly sliced celery

3 cups chopped, peeled baking potatoes

1 tablespoon minced fresh thyme or 1½ teaspoons dried thyme

3½ cups fish broth or 3 cups reduced-sodium chicken broth plus ½ cup bottled clam juice

5 dozen hard-shell clams (see notes below)

Parsley sprigs

2 cups whole milk

2 cups half-and-half

2 cups fresh corn kernels

1 teaspoon kosher salt

1½ teaspoons freshly ground coarse black pepper

3 tablespoons unsalted butter, cut into small chunks

Pinch cayenne pepper

1 cup minced flat-leaf parsley

1. Sauté the bacon in a Dutch oven over medium heat until crisp. Remove with a slotted spoon to paper towels. Add the onions, garlic and celery and sauté in the bacon grease for about 10 minutes, until the onions are softened. Add the potatoes, thyme and broth. Cover and simmer until the potatoes are tender, 10 to 12 minutes.

2. Scrub the clams well. Put them into a large saucepan with 1 cup water and several parsley sprigs. Cover and cook over high heat about 5 minutes, until the clams open. Discard any clams that remain closed. Remove the clams from the shells and roughly chop. Strain the cooking liquid through a cheesecloth and reserve. Save some of the shells for garnish. (The chowder, bacon and clams can be prepared ahead to this point and refrigerated for up to 24 hours. Rewarm the chowder over medium heat before continuing with the recipe.)

3. Reduce the heat to low. Add the milk, half-and-half, bacon, clams and their juice, corn, salt and pepper. Simmer very gently for 3 to 4 minutes just to warm through. Serve with butter, cayenne and parsley on top.

VARIATIONS

White Fish Chowder Substitute 2 pounds whitefish, such as halibut, snapper, turbot or cod, cut into 1½-inch chunks, for the clams. When making a fish chowder, I like to replace the celery with 1½ cups thinly sliced fennel and add ¼ cup dry white wine or vermouth in Step 1. Skip Step 2. The fish will take 8 to 10 minutes to cook in Step 3.

Smoked Fish Chowder In Step 1, decrease the bacon to 4 ounces. You may need to add some additional vegetable oil to the pan to sauté the vegetables. Skip Step 2. In Step 3, replace the clams with 7 ounces (about 1½ cups) flaked smoked trout, salmon or whitefish and delete the salt. For the garnish, replace half of the parsley with chopped fresh dill.

NOTE: If clams in their shells aren't available, use 4 (14-ounce) cans baby clams. Add the clams and their liquid in Step 3 with the other ingredients.

MARVELOUS MOLLUSKS—CLAMS, MUSSELS AND OYSTERS

Clams, mussels and oysters purchased in the shell must be alive with clean, unbroken shells and a fresh "seaside" smell. Live mollusks will close if they are tapped lightly on the countertop; any that do not close should be discarded. If it is necessary to store them, place them in a shallow dish covered loosely with damp towels, fresh seaweed or moistened paper towels and place in the refrigerator (the temperature should be between 38 to 41°F). They should not be stored in a plastic bag or underwater. Use within a day or two.

There are two main types of clams: hard-shell (littlenecks, cherrystones, chowders, quahogs) and soft-shell (long-necks, steamers, razors). Scrub shells thoroughly under cold, running water before opening. Hard-shell clams are generally less sandy than soft-shelled clams and for this reason are often worth the extra cost. If it is necessary to clean clams, they can be soaked for 20 minutes in salt brine made with ⅓ cup salt and one gallon water. Drain and repeat until the clams do not excrete any sand.

Mussels come in dozens of species, but the most available include the blue or common mussel, which has a dark blue shell, and the green-lipped mussel, which has a bright green shell. In addition to scrubbing the shells of mussels (like clams), they should also be debearded shortly before cooking. To debeard mussels, just pull off the wiry, brownish ligament that protrudes from the shell.

Oysters come from the east and west coasts, are both natural and cultivated and include many varieties. When purchasing oysters in the shell they should be alive just like clams and mussels. Oysters are also frequently available shucked, which is a great convenience if they are to be used in a chowder or other recipe. Fresh, shucked oysters should appear plump, consistent in size, have good color and smell fresh. The oyster liquor they are packed in should be clear. Shucked oysters should also be stored in the refrigerator and used within two days.

When preparing mollusks it is important not to overcook them or they will become tough and rubbery. When steaming, cook just until the shells open.

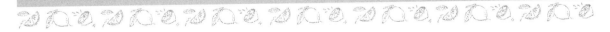

Classic Burgers

Ground meat is the basis of some of the world's most popular dishes: hamburgers, polpettone, moussaka and lasagna to name a few. Everyone has their own version of the perfect hamburger; I've included mine below with cooking tips that I think make a difference. The yummy Lamb Burger variation is an opportunity to include some Middle Eastern spicing at your next barbecue. Turkey burgers have become very popular in recent years, appealing to those looking for a lighter temptation. This recipe produces the moistest turkey burger I've ever had. The Salmon Burger is remarkably tender and moist with a crispy crust.

Most ground meat is labelled according to fat content. Ground beef chuck with 20 percent fat (80 percent lean) makes the most flavorful and moist burgers, while turkey with 10 percent or more fat is the best choice for burgers or other grilled recipes.

You may certainly want to experiment with your own combinations of spicing. Ground meats readily adapt to many different herb, spice and aromatic combinations. Minced parsley, chives, garlic, onions, shallots, green onions, fresh ginger, basil, oregano and minced jalapeños are particularly good. Prepared sauces like Worcestershire, soy and Tabasco add spiciness and moisture. To check a raw mixture for seasoning, cook a teaspoon or so of the seasoned mixture in an oiled pan and then taste. The techniques used to cook ground meats vary, but the one imperative is that the meat is cooked thoroughly. Because of bacteria, ground meat should be served at an internal temperature of 160°F (70°C).

Burgers should be formed into ¼-pound patties about ¾ inch thick. Handle ground meat as little as possible to keep it tender. It is best to turn a burger only once during cooking. The salmon burger should be mixed and chilled for 1 to 2 hours before cooking.

Casual • Quick and Easy • Kid Appeal

PARTY TIME PREPARATIONS: 10 minutes of hands-on cooking.

SERVING EQUIPMENT: Platter, tongs or large fork and condiment bowls.

BEVERAGE TO ACCOMPANY: Beer, Cabernet, Chardonnay

Makes 8 servings

2 pounds ground beef chuck or sirloin (20 percent fat)

4 tablespoons minced onion

2 garlic cloves, minced

2 tablespoons minced fresh oregano

1 teaspoon kosher salt

¼ teaspoon freshly ground coarse black pepper

8 slices Cheddar or Swiss cheese (optional)

8 buns

Lettuce leaves

Tomatoes, sliced

Ketchup, mayonnaise and mustard

1. In a bowl, gently combine ground beef, onion, garlic, oregano, salt and pepper. Form into 8 (¾-inch-thick) patties. Grill over hot coals or cook in a hot skillet for 4 to 5 minutes per side, turning once only.

2. After the turning, top the burgers with the cheese, if desired. Serve on toasted buns with tomato slices, lettuce leaves and condiments.

✹ VARIATIONS

Lamb Burgers

2 pounds ground lamb or 1 pound ground beef chuck and 1 pound ground lamb

2 tablespoons minced Italian parsley

2 teaspoons minced fresh rosemary

¼ cup chopped onion

2 garlic cloves, minced

1 tablespoon fresh lemon juice

1 tablespoon olive oil

1 teaspoon kosher salt

¼ teaspoon freshly ground coarse black pepper

4 ounces kasseri or feta cheese (optional)

8 buns or pita bread

Tomatoes, sliced

Lettuce leaves

Hummus (optional)

1. In a bowl, gently combine the lamb, parsley, rosemary, onion, garlic, lemon juice, oil, salt and pepper. Form into 8 (¾-inch-thick) patties. Grill over hot coals or cook in a hot skillet for 4 to 5 minutes per side, turning once.

2. After turning, top the burgers with the cheese, if desired. Serve on toasted buns with tomato slices, lettuce leaves and hummus, if using.

Salmon Burgers

2 pounds skinless, boneless salmon, cut into 1-inch pieces

1/3 cup mayonnaise

1/2 cup chopped green onions

1 clove garlic, minced

2 teaspoons grated fresh ginger

1 teaspoon sesame oil

1 teaspoon soy sauce

1/4 teaspoon freshly ground coarse black pepper

1 teaspoon kosher salt

Sourdough buns or shepherd's bread

Lettuce leaves

Mayonnaise (page 139), with powdered wasabi or minced jalapeño chile stirred in

1. Grind salmon pieces in a food processor by pulsing until it is a small chop consistency. In a bowl, mix the salmon with mayonnaise, green onions, garlic, ginger, sesame oil, soy sauce and pepper. Cover and chill for 1 to 2 hours.
2. Form into patties and cook in a nonstick skillet over medium-high heat, about 3 minutes per side, until a crispy crust forms. Serve on toasted sourdough buns with lettuce leaves and spicy mayonnaise.

Turkey Burgers

2 pounds ground turkey

4 teaspoons Dijon mustard

1/4 cup bread crumbs

1/4 teaspoon ground cumin

1/4 teaspoon kosher salt

1/4 cup chopped parsley

1 egg white, lightly beaten

1/2 cup minced onion

Brie cheese (optional)

8 buns or rye bread

Tomatoes, sliced

Lettuce leaves

1/2 cup Mayonnaise (page 139), with 2 tablespoons cranberry sauce stirred in

1. In a bowl, mix the turkey, mustard, crumbs, cumin, salt, parsley, egg white and onion together gently in a bowl. Form into patties and cook on a well-oiled grill over hot coals or in a hot skillet, 4 to 5 minutes per side, turning once.
2. Top burgers with cheese, if desired, after the first turn. Serve on toasted buns with tomato slices, lettuce leaves and cranberry mayonnaise.

GRILLED PIZZA

The best news about the proliferation of pizza parlors (other than the ready availability of something to feed the baby-sitter) is that they will often sell you their homemade dough. But even if all you can get is the pizza dough from the Pillsbury tube, you can still make a company-worthy pizza in a flash with the assistance of your grill. A grilled pizza has all the pizzazz of an oven-fired pie along with beautiful grill marks. Gourmet pizza is one of the classic solutions to the problem of what to serve a mixed crowd of kids and adults without making two different menus. Grill the crusts, put out a rainbow selection of toppings and everyone's happy.

PIZZA GRILLING TIPS

Roll out the dough to an 8- to 10-inch circle (any larger is difficult to handle on the grill). Brush with olive oil and place on a hot, very clean grill. Let cook (without moving) for 2 to 3 minutes. When it feels set, flip over and cook for 2 to 3 minutes on the second side. Transfer to a baking pan coated in coarse cornmeal and let cool for later topping, or use immediately.

Once the topping selection has been added, put the pizza back on the grill for a couple of minutes just to melt the cheese or heat through. Voilà, it's a party!

20-Minute Pastas

No man is lonely while eating spaghetti—it requires so much attention.

—Anonymous

Pasta recipes are often prepared from simple ingredients as the centerpiece of a cozy family meal. However, I find that pasta can also be one of the best solutions for last-minute entertaining. This section includes five very easy, very elegant sauces for a variety of pasta shapes. Each of these sauces can be completed in under 20 minutes. They can mostly be made in advance and are each special enough to make the ever-popular pasta into a festive dinner.

Pasta lends itself to satisfying vegetarian meals; three of these recipes are excellent with or without the suggested protein additions. Warm pasta dishes are improved by adding the just-cooked and drained pasta into the sauce while still warm. Plan your pasta timing accordingly, based on the package directions. Cooking times will typically vary from 4 to 6 minutes for fresh pasta and 10 to 14 minutes for dried pasta.

I anticipate these pastas may prove to be some of the most popular dishes in the book. Each of these produces a boldly flavored, beautiful entrée in virtually the time it takes you to cook the pasta. These sauces are also versatile, what you look for in your entertaining repertoire. In each recipe I have indicated their additional uses. Some can be used to enhance a simple (even purchased) baked chicken or fish dish. The Multitude of Mushrooms sauce is great as a filling for hors d'oeuvre tartlets.

Formal • Quick and Easy • Vegetarian Option

PARTY TIME PREPARATIONS: Bake and serve.

SERVING EQUIPMENT: If served on a buffet, a deep platter or bowl with serving tongs or fork and spoon.

BEVERAGE TO ACCOMPANY: Chardonnay, Meursault, Condrieu

Each recipe makes 8 servings

BACON, RADICCHIO AND
WALNUT PASTA

1 pound orecchiette pasta

8 slices thick-cut bacon or 5 ounces sliced pancetta

3 cups shredded radicchio

¾ cup toasted walnut halves or pine nuts

2 teaspoons toasted fennel seeds

½ cup seedless grapes, sliced in half, or dried currants

Kosher salt and freshly ground coarse black pepper, to taste

¾ cup crumbled kasseri cheese

1. Add pasta to a large pot of boiling salted water and cook according to package directions.

2. While the pasta cooks, sauté the bacon in a large pan until crispy. Remove to paper towels to drain. Add the radicchio to the hot fat and sauté until wilted, about 45 seconds. When cool enough to handle, dice the bacon. Add the bacon and all remaining ingredients, except the cheese, back into the pan and toss to mix. Remove from heat.

3. Drain the pasta but do not rinse. Add the pasta to the sauté pan; toss with the bacon mixture. Taste and season with salt and pepper as desired. Sprinkle with cheese and serve immediately.

Cold Asian Sesame Noodles

6 tablespoons toasted sesame oil	½ teaspoon red chile pepper flakes
¼ cup tahini or smooth peanut butter	1 teaspoon chili oil
¼ cup soy sauce	2 (10-ounce packages) Chinese wheat or egg noodles
2 tablespoons water	
4 teaspoons minced garlic	3 cups slivered snow peas (about ½ pound)
2½ tablespoons minced fresh ginger	3 cups diced red bell pepper (about 1 pound)
¼ cup seasoned rice vinegar	1 cup chopped fresh cilantro
4 teaspoons sugar	2 tablespoons toasted sesame seeds
1 to 2 teaspoons Chinese chili paste (use the larger amount for a spicier flavor)	3 to 4 cups shredded roast chicken, cooked shrimp or grilled tofu (optional)

1. **TO MAKE THE DRESSING:** In a blender or small food processor, mix all the ingredients from the sesame oil to the chili oil to a smooth consistency. This can be prepared and held in the refrigerator for up to 3 days.

2. Cook the noodles in a pot of boiling water according to package directions. Drain in a colander and rinse under cold water. Drain again and toss with the snow peas and bell pepper.

3. **TO SERVE:** Drizzle on the sesame dressing and toss to coat. Sprinkle with the cilantro and sesame seeds. For a main course, add the chicken and toss to combine.

A Multitude of Mushrooms and Cream Pasta

1 pound fettucine or tagliarini

½ cup olive oil

3 tablespoons unsalted butter

3 cloves garlic, minced

8 cups (about 18 ounces) sliced fresh mushrooms (shiitake, porcini, portobello, cremini or white button)

3 tablespoons minced fresh thyme

1 teaspoon salt

¾ cup dry vermouth

3 tablespoons mushroom powder (see note, below)

¼ teaspoon freshly grated nutmeg

1½ cups whipping cream

3 tablespoons grated lemon zest

4 ounces chèvre (a mild, creamy goat cheese is best)

Freshly ground coarse black pepper

¾ cup chopped parsley

½ cup shaved Parmesan cheese plus extra for the table

1. Cook pasta according to package directions.
2. While the pasta cooks, heat the olive oil and butter in a large sauté pan over medium-high heat. Add the garlic and sauté 2 minutes. Add the mushrooms, thyme and salt and sauté until the mushrooms are softened, about 6 minutes. Stir in the vermouth, mushroom powder and nutmeg and simmer for 2 minutes. Add cream and lemon zest and simmer 3 to 4 minutes to thicken. Finally, add the chèvre and cook, stirring, until melted and creamy. Add freshly ground black pepper to taste. The sauce can be made up to 1 day ahead, refrigerated and gently reheated.
3. **TO SERVE:** Drain pasta, but do not rinse. Transfer to a platter or individual plates and spoon sauce over the top. Garnish with chopped parsley and Parmesan cheese. Serve additional Parmesan on the side.

NOTE: Make mushroom powder by grinding dried mushrooms (shiitake, porcini or morels) in a small grinder, such as a cleaned coffee grinder, until a fine powder is formed. One ounce of dried mushrooms makes 5 tablespoons powder. Extra mushroom powder can be stored in an airtight container in the freezer.

Shrimp with Vodka Tomato Sauce

(This recipe takes a little longer than 20 minutes because the shrimp needs to marinate.)

2½ pounds medium or large shrimp, peeled, deveined and rinsed

½ cup olive oil

2 teaspoons kosher salt

2 tablespoons minced garlic

1 fresh red Thai or serrano chile, seeded and sliced

½ teaspoon freshly ground coarse black pepper

1 pound dried fusilli pasta

3 tablespoons unsalted butter

3 cans (14½ ounces each) diced tomatoes

2 bay leaves

2 tablespoons vodka

1 tablespoon grated lemon zest

⅓ cup sliced fresh mint

½ cup sliced fresh basil

¼ cup chopped watercress or Italian parsley

1. Combine the shrimp, olive oil, 1 teaspoon of the kosher salt, minced garlic, chile and black pepper in a bowl or resealable plastic bag. Marinate for 1 to 4 hours in the refrigerator.
2. Cook pasta according to package directions.
3. While the pasta cooks, heat a large skillet over medium-high heat. Add half of the shrimp, including half of the marinade, to the pan and sauté 4 to 5 minutes, until the shrimp are firm and pink. Remove the shrimp to a large bowl. Cook the remaining shrimp and marinade and add to the bowl. Add the butter to the bowl and toss together.
4. Turn the heat down to medium under the sauté pan and add the tomatoes, bay leaves and remaining 1 teaspoon salt. Simmer gently for 5 minutes. Add the vodka and lemon zest and bring to a boil for 60 seconds. Remove from the heat, stir in the mint and basil and let rest 3 to 4 minutes.
5. **TO SERVE:** Drain pasta, but do not rinse. Add the pasta to the bowl with the shrimp and toss to mix. Add the tomato sauce and toss. Sprinkle with the watercress. Serve immediately.

Asparagus Festival Fettucine

2 pounds young asparagus, trimmed of woody ends, cut into 1-inch pieces

4 tablespoons unsalted butter

2 tablespoons mashed garlic

⅓ cup fresh lemon juice

1⅓ cups chicken broth

⅓ cup dry vermouth

1½ cups whipping cream

1 teaspoon freshly ground coarse black pepper

1 pound fettucine

½ cup chopped Italian parsley

2 tablespoons capers, drained

Sautéed scallops, poached salmon or boneless chicken breast (optional)

⅓ cup freshly grated Parmesan cheese, plus more for the table

1. Bring a large pot of salted water to a boil. Put the asparagus pieces in a strainer or pasta basket and submerge in the boiling water for 60 seconds. Remove, leaving the pot of hot water on the stove. Drain the asparagus and cool under cold water. Set aside.

2. Meanwhile, heat 2 tablespoons of the butter in a large sauté pan over medium-high heat. When the butter is sizzling, add the mashed garlic. Sauté the garlic until softened and aromatic, about 3 minutes, being careful not to brown. Add the lemon juice, chicken broth and vermouth. Raise the heat to high, bring to a boil and reduce by half, about 12 minutes. Whisk in the cream and black pepper; boil until reduced to a sauce consistency, about 10 minutes. (The sauce and asparagus can be prepared to here up to one day ahead. If prepared in advance, gently reheat before proceeding.)

3. Cook the pasta according to directions on package.

4. Reduce the heat under the sauce to medium, add the parsley and capers and simmer for 3 to 4 minutes to blend. Remove from the heat and whisk in the remaining 2 tablespoons butter. Stir in the asparagus. Let the sauce rest for 2 minutes to warm the asparagus before tossing with the pasta. Add the scallops, if using, and toss to combine. Sprinkle with the Parmesan cheese and serve immediately.

Roasting Charts

In my experience, clever food is not appreciated at Christmas. It makes the little ones cry and the old ones nervous.

—Sir Oliver Wendell Holmes, Sr.

Your recipe collection is dramatically expanded with the roasting charts that follow. They provide all the necessary information for roasting the cuts of meat, poultry and fish that are most popular for entertaining.

Here are some general tips to make roasting more successful:

- Always bring the meat or fish to room temperature before putting it into the oven.

- Some cuts are improved with a dry rub or marinade.

- The perfect roasting pan is made of heavy metal with sides that are no more than ¾ of the height of the roast.

- After removing from the oven let a 3- to 4-pound roast or whole chicken rest for 10 to 15 minutes before carving; let a 7- to 8-pound roast or whole turkey rest 15 to 25 minutes before carving. This keeps all of the tasty juices in the meat and not on your cutting board.

- When possible, have the butcher leave at least ¼ inch of fat on all meats to be roasted.

- Many of the recipes have 2 temperatures suggested—first to sear and then to roast. For a large piece of meat the initial high heat that is necessary to sear (or brown) the exterior of the roast must be lowered to allow for the time required to cook the meat through. For small pieces of meat, like a pork tenderloin, the searing period will also cook the meat to medium-rare or desired doneness.

- There is a 5 to 10 degree difference in the recommended temperature to remove a roast from the oven and the ideal serving temperature. This allows for the increase in internal temperature that will take place while the roast sets before carving.

Roasts often yield a sticky, bottom-of-the-pan residue, which is the backbone for delicious "deglazed" or "pan" sauces (fattier roasts yield thicker pan juices). A pan sauce is the quickest way to make a sauce to accompany roasted meat or poultry. They can adapt to an unlimited number of flavor combinations and provide an easy finishing touch once you understand the technique. Follow these steps to create delicious pan sauces:

1. Remove the roast from the roasting pan.

2. Spoon off any excess fat and put the pan over medium-high heat.

3. Quickly pour in some wine, water, juice or broth. The liquid will sizzle and in the process dissolve the browned bits from the pan, adding that rich flavor to the liquid. This is called deglazing and is the beginning of a sauce. Stir with a spoon to make sure all bits are dislodged.

4. At this point other flavor ingredients like fresh or dried herbs, sautéed vegetables or dried fruit may be added. Additional broth or other liquid may also be needed. The sauce should be simmered for a few minutes to a nice consistency. Before serving stir in a little butter, salt and pepper to taste.

Some easy pan sauces might include a mushroom Madeira sauce to be served with beef. Use the Madeira to deglaze. Add sautéed cremini or other flavorful mushrooms, a little beef broth and simmer. Finish with a nub of unsalted butter, salt and pepper.

A Shiraz rosemary sauce would pair beautifully with lamb. Deglaze the pan with some Shiraz wine. Add some minced fresh rosemary and a little beef or chicken broth and finish as above.

A thyme cherry sauce would highlight an entrée of pork or duck. Deglaze the pan with sherry. Add minced fresh thyme, some dried cherries and chicken broth and simmer. Finish once again with butter, salt and pepper. There are many variations to make pan sauces. These are just a few to get you started.

 # Poultry

Poultry is the most universally popular entrée. It is lean, economical and suited to virtually any kind of preparation. The challenge when cooking poultry is to achieve golden, crisp skin and a moist, but thoroughly cooked interior. This can be handled by starting the bird on high heat to brown and seal in the juices (searing), then reducing the oven temperature to cook the meat through. In addition to checking the temperature of your bird with an instant-read thermometer in the thickest part of the thigh, you can test for doneness by pricking the thigh. When the juices run clear (no red or pink) the meat is done. Because the white meat on chicken and turkey cooks more quickly than dark meat, aluminum foil may need to be placed over the breast while the dark meat of the leg finishes cooking. Duck, on the other hand, is quite fatty and cooks at a more consistent rate since the meat is all dark. When roasting a whole duck, thoroughly prick the skin (being careful not to go through to the flesh) especially over the breast. This will help drain as much fat as possible from the bird. The skin should roast to a crispy, rich brown color while the flesh in the breast remains slightly pink.

CUT OR TYPE, NUMBER OF SERVINGS	OVEN TEMPERATURE	MINUTES PER POUND	INTERNAL TEMPERATURE	HERBS, SPICES, SAUCES
Chicken (whole roaster), 4 to 7 lbs. Serves 2 to 4	Sear 425°F (220°C) Cook 325°F (165°C)	About 12 to 15 minutes; add 15 to 20 minutes if stuffed	Test thigh and remove from oven at 160°F (70°C); serve at 170°F (75°C)	Cumin, garlic, lemon, parsley, pomegranate, tarragon, thyme, white wine, A Multitude of Mushrooms and Cream Sauce (page 117)
Cornish game hen 1 to 1½ lbs. Serves 1	350°F (180°C)	About 18 minutes	Test thigh and remove from oven at 160°F (70°C); serve at 170°F (75°C)	Marjoram, mustard, oregano, rosemary, thyme, white wine, Curry-Coconut Sauce (page 146)
Turkey (whole, stuffed) average 13–18 lbs. Serving-1 lb	Sear 425°F (220°C)	About 15 minutes	Test thigh and remove from oven at 160°F (70°C); serve at 170°F (75°C)	Celery, chestnuts, maple syrup, parsley, sage, sausage, tarragon, thyme, white wine
Turkey breast roast (bone in) 4½ to 6 lbs. 6 to 8 oz. per person	Cook 325°F (165°C) 450°F (230°C)	About 15 minutes per pound	Remove from oven at 140°F (60°C); serve at 150°F (65°C)	Lemon, marsala, mushrooms, parsley, tarragon, thyme, white wine marinades
Long Island duck (whole) 4 to 5 lbs. Serves 2 to 3	Sear 425°F (220°C) for 30 minutes Cook 350°F (180°C)	About 15 minutes per pound	Test thigh and remove from oven at 160°F (70°C); serve at 170°F (75°C)	Apples, cherries, garlic, gin, ginger, honey, orange, paprika, pomegranate, molasses, sherry, soy sauce, Balsamic Blueberry Sauce (page 77)

Fish

A whole roasted fish makes an elegant presentation for a party. Be sure to have your fishmonger clean the fish, removing the scales, guts and fins, but leave the head and tail on. Some types of fish may be too large to serve whole and in these cases a large "center cut" will work well, too. Each of these fish benefits from a moist filling of some type tucked into the belly cavity. This can be as simple as a bundle of fresh herbs and lemon slices. More complex fillings might include crabmeat, herbs, bread crumbs, sliced fennel, mushrooms and scallions. Keep the belly closed with toothpicks or short skewers and brush the outside of the fish with a light coating of vegetable oil. To check for doneness in a large piece of fish insert a thin-bladed knife into the thickest part. If the knife inserts without resistance and the flesh appears almost opaque, the fish is done. Allow the fish to rest about 10 minutes. It will continue to cook while it rests. The cooked flesh should appear opaque, yet moist.

CUT OR TYPE, NUMBER OF SERVINGS	OVEN TEMPERATURE	COOKING TIME	DONENESS TEST	HERBS, SPICES, SAUCES
Whole salmon (if large, use center cut, skin on) 8 to 10 oz. per serving	475°F (245°C)	10 minutes per inch of thickness, measured at thickest point of fish	Check center of fish; should be tender and almost opaque	Basil, cilantro, dill, ginger, hollandaise, lemon, parsley, shallots, tarragon, white wine, Curry-Coconut Sauce (page 146)
Whole red snapper 3 to 5 lbs. 8 to 10 oz. per serving	475°F (245°C)	10 minutes per inch of thickness, measured at thickest point of fish	Check center of fish; should be tender and almost opaque	Capers, ginger, green olives, lemon, marjoram, mustard, oregano, tomatoes, Salsa Rustica (page 141)
Albacore (center cut, skin removed, about 3 inches thick) 6 to 8 oz. per serving	475°F (245°C)	10 minutes per inch of thickness, measured at thickest point of fish	Check center of fish; should be tender and almost opaque	Basil, garlic, ginger, lemon, lime, mirin, onions, sesame, soy, Sesame-Ginger Mayonnaise (page 140)
Halibut (center cut, deboned, skin removed) 6 to 8 oz. per serving	475°F (245°C)	10 minutes per inch of thickness, measured at thickest point of fish	Check center of fish; should be tender and almost opaque	Lemon, orange, parsley, red bell pepper, saffron, white wine, Lavender Mayonnaise (page 140)
Swordfish (center cut, deboned, skin on) 6 to 8 oz. per serving	475°F (245°C)	10 minutes per inch of thickness, measured at thickest point of fish	Check center of fish; should be tender and almost opaque	Basil, capers, garlic, parsley, tomatoes, Avocado-Chipotle Salsa (page 144)
Whole striped bass 8 to 10 oz. per serving	475°F (245°C)	10 minutes per inch of thickness, measured at thickest point of fish	Check center of fish; should be tender and almost opaque	Fennel, lemon, shallots, tarragon, white wine, Basil-Mint Pesto (page 138)
Whole pompano 2 to 3 lbs. 8 to 10 oz. per serving	475°F (245°C)	10 minutes per inch of thickness, measured at thickest point of fish	Check center of fish; should be tender and almost opaque	Basil, lemon, lime, mustard, Herb Sauce from Crab Cakes (page 6)

 # Beef

There is nothing easier or more elegant for entertaining than a perfectly roasted piece of beef. Holiday dinners around the world have centered on standing rib roasts. A whole tenderloin is one of the most elegant entrées for a special dinner party. The tri-tip, an economic but extremely flavorful cut of meat, can adapt to ethnic marinades and become a festive centerpiece for a party.

It is imperative when serving large cuts of meat to let them rest after removing from the oven before carving. The internal temperature will rise about 10 degrees while the flavorful meat juices are drawn back into the meat. Large cuts of meat should be seared at a high temperature to impart a rich brown crust, but should finish cooking at a lower temperature until done. Smaller cuts of meat can be cooked continuously at a high temperature until done.

CUT OR TYPE, NUMBER OF SERVINGS	OVEN TEMPERATURE	MINUTES PER POUND	INTERNAL TEMPERATURE	HERBS, SPICES, SAUCES
Standing rib roast (prime rib) 3 ribs = 8 portions; 4 ribs = 10 to 12 portions	Sear 450°F (230°C) Cook 325 to 350°F (165 to 180°C)	15 minutes per pound	For rare, remove from oven at 125°F (50°C); serve at 135°F (55°C) For medium-rare, remove from oven at 130°F (55°C); serve at 140°F (60°C)	Mushrooms, rosemary, thyme, Horseradish-Dijon Butter (page 74)
Top sirloin roast (N.Y. Strip) 8 to 10 lbs. 8 oz. portion	Sear 450°F (230°C) Cook 350°F (180°C)	15 minutes per pound	For rare, remove from oven at 125°F (50°C); serve at 135°F (55°C) For medium-rare, remove from oven at 130°F (55°C); serve 140°F (60°C)	Chervil, garlic, red wine, thyme, Gorgonzola Cream Sauce (page 146)
Tenderloin (whole fillet) 4 lbs. 7- to 8-oz. portions	450°F (230°C)	10 to 12 minutes per pound	For rare, remove from oven at 125°F (50°C); serve at 135°F (55°C) For medium-rare, remove from oven at 130°F (55°C); serve at 140°F (60°C)	Madeira, shallots, thyme, truffles, Compound Butters (page 145)
Tri-tip roast* 1½ to 2½ lbs. 6- to 8-oz. portions	450°F (230°C) (Lower temperature to 350°F [180°C] if a sweet rub is used)	15 minutes per pound	For rare, remove from oven at 125°F (50°C); serve at 135°F (55°C) For medium-rare, remove from oven at 130°F (55°C); serve at 140°F (60°C)	Purchased dry rubs (Southwestern, Creole, garlic and herb)

*Indicates that a cut is improved with a dry rub or marinade.

Lamb

In ancient times a whole roasted lamb was used to celebrate rituals and life passage occasions, and it is still a favorite food for celebrations all over the world. Lamb has a distinctive, delicately gamy, slightly sweet flavor, which lends itself to stronger mixtures of herbs and spices than beef. Because of this, many lamb dishes have pronounced ethnic flavors. Greek souvlaki, Moroccan tagine, French gigot d'agneau and the Indian Rogan Josh among many others. Lamb is particularly complemented by rosemary, garlic, red wine, yogurt, coriander, oregano, curry, mint and mustard. Lamb is best when served still pink. Remember, the temperature will rise about 10 degrees while the roast rests before carving.

CUT OR TYPE, NUMBER OF SERVINGS	OVEN TEMPERATURE	MINUTES PER POUND	INTERNAL TEMPERATURE	HERBS, SPICES, SAUCES
Boneless leg 3 to 4½ lbs. 8-oz. portions	400°F (205°C)	About 15 minutes per pound	For rare, remove from oven at 125°F (50°C); serve at 135°F (55°C) For medium-rare, remove from oven at 130°F (55°C); serve at 140°F (60°C)	Garlic, harissa sauce, lemon, mint, mustard, onions, parsley, pomegranates, red wine, rosemary, thyme, yogurt
Leg of lamb (bone in) 6 to 8 lbs. 8 to 12 servings	Sear 425°F (220°C) Cook 350°F (180°C)	About 12 to 15 minutes per pound	For rare, remove from oven at 125°F (50°C); serve at 135°F (55°C) For medium-rare, remove from oven at 130°F (55°C); serve at 140°F (60°C)	Garlic, lemon, mint, mustard, onions, parsley, pomegranates, red wine, rosemary, thyme, yogurt, Shiraz Rosemary Pan Sauce (see page 121)
Rack (a rack has 7 to 8 ribs) 1 rack for 2 persons	450°F (205°C) Meaty side up in shallow pan	15 to 20 minutes total cooking time	For rare, remove from oven at 125°F (50°C); serve at 135°F (55°C) For medium-rare, remove from oven at 130°F (55°C); serve at 140°F (60°C)	Garlic, mint, mustard, rosemary, thyme. Rub liberally with the Basil-Mint Pesto (page 138) and coat meaty topside with cornmeal.

 # Pork

Pork has been popular for celebrations since Roman times. Its sweet, mild flavor and juicy texture has proven to be a great foil for bright spices, fruits and herbs in every cuisine, with the exception of Muslim and Jewish communities. At your butcher, look for meat that is pale pink with a small amount of marbling and white fat (the older the pork, the darker pink the meat). Due to changes in diet, pork today has about one-third less fat than only ten years ago. Because of this, many of the cooking procedures used for poultry are appropriate for the leanest cuts of pork. In the past there was concern about thoroughly cooking pork to kill trichinosis. Pigs today are raised in an exceptionally clean environment and this has not been a problem for many years. If pork is removed from the oven at 140°F (60°C), the meat will be safe from any possibility of contamination, but not dried out. The pork removed from the oven at these temperatures will be cooked to medium-rare and appear slightly pink and moist.

CUT OR TYPE, NUMBER OF SERVINGS	OVEN TEMPERATURE	MINUTES PER POUND	INTERNAL TEMPERATURE	HERBS, SPICES, SAUCES
Boneless loin roast (center cut) 3½ to 4½ lbs. 6 to 7 oz. per person	375°F (190°C)	About 20 minutes per pound	Remove from oven at 140°F (60°C); serve at 150°F (65°C)	Apples, cognac, currants, ginger, oranges, pineapple, prunes, Thyme Cherry Pan Sauce (see page 121)
Spareribs* Slabs can weigh 2 to 3 lbs. 12 to 16 oz. per person	300°F (150°C), covered to cook fork tender 500°F (260°C), uncovered, 10 minutes to crisp	1½ hours or until fork tender		Barbecue sauce, chili powder, cumin, hoisin sauce, honey, pineapple, star anise, whiskey
Tenderloin ¾ to 1¼ lbs. 6 to 7 oz. per person	450°F (230°C)	12 to 15 minutes total cooking time	Remove from oven at 140 to 145°F (60 to 65°C); serve at 150 to 155°F (65 to 70°C)	Curry powder, garlic, mustard, onion, shallots, sherry, Balsamic Blueberry Sauce (page 77)
Ham (fully cooked, bone in) Whole 10 to 20 lbs., often available in shank or butt halves 8 to 10 oz. per person	325°F (165°C)	About 15 minutes per pound	Remove from oven at 130°F (55°C); serve at 140°F (60°C)	Apples, brown sugar, cloves, honey mustard sauce, mustard, orange, pineapple, port wine

*Indicates that a cut is improved with a dry rub or marinade.

Marinades, Sauces and Salad Dressings

The remarkable thing about my mother is that for thirty years she served us nothing but leftovers. The original meal has never been found.
—Calvin Trillin

SAUCES AND DRESSINGS ARE THE ties that bind disparate flavors together and add flair to simple preparations. Without dressing a salad would just be a bowl of unrelated vegetables; dressing gives them a common language. Bold sauces enliven mild dishes; without an exciting sauce, a simple roast isn't quite dressed for company. The beautiful color and sheen of a sauce also contributes to the appeal of your plate.

This chapter includes some of the most versatile recipes in the book. The bright vinaigrettes can be used to dress a green or pasta salad or flavor roasted vegetables. With slight variation, they can be used to marinate skewered meat for grilling. The subtly flavored mayonnaises can be used to add zing to a gourmet sandwich, your mom's devilled eggs, a memorable potato salad or steamed vegetables.

Like so many other flavors introduced from the Italian kitchen, pestos have proven themselves to be a flexible preparation that appeals to nearly everyone. I have included quite a variety, and I'm sure you'll come up with many more. Made thick, they are excellent used to stuff a roast leg of lamb or pork loin. Made a little thinner and you have a quick pasta sauce, spread for crostini or sauce for steamed vegetables. Mixed with a mild cheese, pestos create lovely dips and spreads for crudité and crackers.

The chapter concludes with some elegant cream sauces. They reflect the current trend toward sauces thickened by reduced stock or cream instead of the traditional flour-based roux. These are very quick and easy; all can be prepared in advance. You will find many, many uses on your party menus for these recipes, turning a simple roast chicken or grilled steak or fish into a dish fit for company.

Marinades

Marinades employ intense concentrations of flavor to infuse the meat, fish or vegetables immersed in them. Often marinades also include some acidic component, like wine or lemon juice, which serves to tenderize while flavoring. Once raw meat has contaminated the marinade, it shouldn't be used as a sauce for the cooked meat unless it has been first heated to a boil.

Red Wine Marinade

Makes about 3½ cups

1½ cups extra-virgin olive oil

1 cup red wine, such as Merlot or Cabernet

1 cup fresh lemon juice

6 tablespoons minced fresh rosemary

4 tablespoons minced garlic

6 tablespoons minced parsley

3 teaspoons kosher salt

1 teaspoon ground cumin

2 teaspoons red chile flakes

2 teaspoons freshly ground coarse black pepper

Combine all ingredients in a bowl or resealable plastic bag. Use for lamb or beef roast or brochettes.

Honey-Ginger Asian Marinade

Makes about 2½ cups

1 cup dry sherry

3 tablespoons minced garlic

3 fresh Thai chiles, chopped

⅓ cup honey, light brown sugar or molasses

3 tablespoons seasoned rice vinegar

⅓ cup soy sauce

¼ cup minced fresh ginger

3 tablespoons sesame oil

2 star anise or 1 cinnamon stick

Combine all ingredients in a bowl or resealable plastic bag. Use for chicken, shrimp or pork.

Greek Marinade

Makes about 3 cups

Peel of 3 lemons, chopped

½ cup plus 2 tablespoons fresh lemon juice

1¾ cups olive oil

¼ cup minced fresh oregano

4 bay leaves

3 tablespoons minced garlic

½ cup white wine

1½ teaspoons kosher salt

¾ teaspoon freshly ground coarse black pepper

Combine all ingredients in a bowl or resealable plastic bag. Use for seafood or chicken.

Vinaigrettes

Vinaigrette, the creamy blending of vinegar, oil and seasonings, is one of the four mother sauces in French classic cuisine. With the addition of fresh herbs, mustard, sugar or honey, and maybe citrus juice in place of vinegar, you can create an endless palette of dressings. I use vinaigrettes, from sweet to sour to creamy, to dress pasta salads, brush on a salmon fillet before broiling or mix with feta for a quick hors d'oeuvre. All of this is in addition to its most traditional use, dressing salads of every hue.

Sherry Vinaigrette

Makes about 1 cup

⅓ cup sherry vinegar

2 teaspoons Dijon mustard

1 shallot, minced

2 large cloves garlic, minced

Pinch kosher salt

Freshly ground coarse black pepper

Pinch sugar

⅔ cup extra-virgin olive oil

1½ tablespoons shredded fresh basil (optional)

1. In a blender, combine all ingredients except oil and basil until smooth. Slowly add the oil with the motor running to emulsify and thicken. Stir in basil, if using.
2. Serve on carrots, baby greens and poached salmon or endive and pear.

Roquefort Vinaigrette

Makes about 1 cup

⅓ cup fresh lemon juice

1 tablespoon white wine vinegar

1 teaspoon freshly ground coarse black pepper

1 tablespoon minced garlic

2 teaspoons chopped fresh oregano

½ teaspoon dried thyme

¼ to ½ teaspoon sugar

¾ cup extra-virgin olive oil

5 to 6 tablespoons crumbled Roquefort cheese

1 chopped, seeded, peeled tomato (optional)

1. Puree the lemon juice, vinegar, pepper, garlic, herbs and sugar in a blender or mini food processor. Slowly add the oil with the motor running to emulsify and thicken.
2. To finish, either whisk in the crumbled cheese or, for a creamier dressing, add the cheese to the blender and pulse briefly to break it down, leaving some chunks. Stir in tomato, if using.

3. Serve on steamed broccoli, fresh mushroom and corn salad, roast beets or hearts of romaine with pepitas and tomato.

Tahini-Lemon Vinaigrette

Makes 1 cup

⅓ cup tahini

⅓ cup fresh lemon juice

2 tablespoons red wine vinegar

1 tablespoon minced garlic

1 teaspoon ground cumin

½ teaspoon honey

1 to 2 tablespoons water

½ teaspoon kosher salt

Pinch cayenne pepper

2 tablespoons extra-virgin olive oil

2 tablespoons minced fresh cilantro or mint

¼ cup diced red bell pepper

1. In a blender, blend the tahini, lemon juice, vinegar, garlic, cumin, honey, water, salt and cayenne until smooth. Slowly add the oil with the motor running to emulsify and thicken. Stir in the cilantro and bell pepper. For a spicier flavor, replace the bell pepper with minced serrano.

2. Serve on grilled eggplant; falafel salad; white bean, fennel and albacore salad; chicken-walnut-nectarine salad; bulgur salad or roast chicken.

Caesar Dressing

Makes 1½ cups

6 anchovy fillets packed in olive oil, drained

4 teaspoons minced garlic (about 8 cloves garlic)

2 egg yolks, preferably pasteurized (see note page 135)

2 tablespoons fresh lemon juice

¼ cup sherry or white wine vinegar

2 teaspoons Worcestershire sauce

1 teaspoon Dijon mustard

1 teaspoon kosher salt

4 drops hot pepper sauce

Freshly ground coarse black pepper

½ cup extra-virgin olive oil

1. Combine all the ingredients except the oil in a food processor. Pulse to puree and blend. With the motor running, slowly add the oil to emulsify and thicken.

2. This is better if made several hours before using. It will keep for up to 3 days in the refrigerator. Serve on the classic Caesar salad and as a dip for crudité.

Evan's Tangerine Vinaigrette

Makes about 1 cup

1 tablespoon minced garlic	1 tablespoon grated lime zest
1 tablespoon minced shallot	½ cup plus 2 tablespoons tangerine juice
¼ cup fresh orange juice	1½ tablespoons fresh lemon juice
1 tablespoon grated orange zest	2 tablespoons sugar
3 to 4 tablespoons grated lime juice	¾ cup extra-virgin olive oil

1. Combine all the ingredients except the oil and whisk to blend and dissolve the sugar. Slowly whisk in the oil to emulsify and thicken.

2. This is better if made a day before using. It will keep for up to 2 weeks in the refrigerator. Serve on a fennel and orange salad, Asian-style cold rice salad or endive, berry and Brie salad.

NOTE: Uncooked eggs should not be eaten by young children, the elderly, or anyone with a compromised immune system, because they may contain salmonella bacteria that can cause serious illness. Pasteurized eggs are available in some markets and are safe to eat in sauces or desserts that are not cooked.

Combine the following dry spices to flavor simple steamed, grilled or roast dishes for those avoiding salt. (These are so tasty I've found that everyone enjoys them.)

Blend for Cooked Vegetables

3 tablespoons toasted sesame seeds	1 teaspoon ground cumin
2 tablespoons dried oregano	½ teaspoon cayenne pepper
2 tablespoons dried sage	½ teaspoon ground ginger
1 tablespoon dried basil	1 teaspoon garlic powder
2 teaspoons dried thyme	1 to 2 tablespoons Dr. Bronner's vegetable powder (optional)
2 teaspoons freshly ground coarse black pepper	

Combine all the ingredients in a small bowl. Store in an airtight container. Drizzle vegetables with a generous amount of fresh lemon juice before seasoning.

Cajun-Style Blend for Seafood, Chicken or Pork

2 tablespoons paprika	1 tablespoon ground cumin
1 teaspoon white pepper	2 tablespoons onion powder
1½ tablespoons garlic powder	1 tablespoon dried oregano
1 teaspoon cayenne pepper	1 teaspoon sugar
2 tablespoons dried thyme	1 tablespoon ground coriander

Combine all the ingredients in a small bowl. Store in an airtight container. Drizzle shrimp or fish with a generous amount of fresh lemon juice before seasoning.

Basil Pesto

Pesto, the uncooked sauce that made Genoa famous, can be one of the most versatile sauces in your kitchen. The classic is based on lots of fresh basil; however, you can successfully use almost any herb, from mint to cilantro, to invent your own. Pesto is a nearly instant sauce for pasta, hot or cold. It can also add herbaceous sparkle to pizza, grilled chicken and fish,

Savory Blend

1 tablespoon ground sage	1 tablespoon fennel seeds
1 tablespoon dried thyme	2 tablespoons onion powder
½ tablespoon ground rosemary	1 teaspoon curry powder
1 teaspoon dry mustard	1 teaspoon sugar
2 tablespoons granulated garlic	
1 tablespoon freshly ground coarse black pepper	

Combine all the ingredients in a small bowl. Store in an airtight container. Use on steak, lamb chops or pork tenderloin.

macaroni and cheese or a simple baked potato. I add pesto to cream cheese for a dip and to purchased soup to brighten the stock. Though good-quality sauces are available now in grocery stores, pesto is so easy to make it's still worth the time to perfect some personal variations.

To make any of these pestos into a sauce consistency, add three or more tablespoons of cream or full-fat yogurt to the finished recipe and warm over low heat. All pestos should ideally rest in the refrigerator for at least 1 hour before serving. Lay a sheet of plastic wrap across the pesto and gently press onto the surface to keep oxygen from discoloring the surface. Don't add salt until the flavors have had a chance to blend for at least that hour.

Makes about 1 cup

2 tablespoons chopped garlic	½ cup freshly grated Parmesan cheese
½ cup pine nuts or almonds, toasted (see note, page 138)	1 teaspoon fresh lemon juice
⅓ to ½ cup extra-virgin olive oil	½ teaspoon white pepper
2 cups loosely packed, chopped fresh basil leaves	Kosher salt, to taste

1. Put the garlic, nuts, half of the oil and the basil into a food processor and pulse to puree. Scrape the sides down occasionally so the ingredients are thoroughly blended. Add the Parmesan cheese, lemon juice, remaining oil and pepper. Pulse to puree, scraping down the sides as necessary.

2. Cover and refrigerate. Season with salt before using. If it will be held for a day or more before serving, press plastic wrap to the surface of the pesto before covering the container. This will help avoid browning. Pesto tastes best if prepared 3 to 4 hours before serving and will last for up to 1 week in the refrigerator.

✺ VARIATIONS

Basil-Mint Pesto Replace 1 cup of the basil with 1 cup chopped fresh mint and reduce the Parmesan cheese to ¼ cup.

Arugula Pesto Replace the basil with 2 cups chopped fresh arugula and increase the lemon juice to 2 tablespoons. The Parmesan cheese can be replaced with ½ cup crumbled aged feta cheese.

Cilantro Pesto Replace the basil with 2½ cups cilantro leaves (no stems) or 2 cups cilantro and ½ cup parsley leaves. Decrease the pine nuts and Parmesan cheese to ¼ cup each (pepitas are also good in place of the pine nuts). Replace the lemon juice with 1 tablespoon fresh lime juice. Add 1 tablespoon minced serrano or jalapeño chile, if desired.

> NOTE: Toast nuts in a dry skillet over medium heat for 3 to 5 minutes, stirring frequently, until browned and aromatic, or toast in a 350°F (180°C) oven. Nuts burn quickly so they should be watched carefully.

Mayonnaise

A flavored mayonnaise is one of the easiest ways to add sophistication to a simple piece of grilled fish, steamed vegetables or even a sandwich buffet. You can also make a pasta, chicken or seafood salad special with any of the following sauces. Brushing mayonnaise on fish fillets before grilling or baking keeps them moist and tender. Made in a food processor, as directed here, mayonnaise is virtually foolproof. Use very fresh, top-quality ingredients and you can create a delicate dressing that will impress everyone with its complex flavor. Everybody likes mayo. Wait till they taste the real thing!

The zesty Lemon Parmesan Aïoli livens up a pasta salad, cold boiled potatoes, poached shrimp or grilled fish. The Lavender Mayonnaise is astonishing on steamed asparagus. Rouille is designed to complement seafood and is also great stirred into a winter soup. Sesame-Ginger Mayonnaise is wonderful on crab cakes or as the basis of a special chicken salad.

Mayonnaise can be held in the refrigerator for up to 4 days. Store it in a tightly sealed container; never use aluminum foil as it will discolor the sauce.

Makes 1½ cups

2 egg yolks plus 1 egg, pasteurized if available (see note, page 135), room temperature

2 teaspoons Dijon mustard

2 teaspoons white wine vinegar or fresh lemon juice

½ teaspoon kosher salt

1¼ to 1½ cups very fresh, top-quality safflower or canola oil

Pinch white pepper

1. Place the egg yolks, egg and mustard in a food processor and blend until well mixed, 15 to 20 seconds.
2. Add the vinegar and salt and blend 7 to 10 seconds.
3. With the motor running, drizzle in the oil very slowly. After the first ¼ cup has been incorporated and the mayonnaise has begun to thicken, you may pour the oil in more quickly. After about 1¼ cups have been added, stop the food processor and test for thickness. From this point on, as you add more oil the mayonnaise becomes thicker.

▒ VARIATIONS

Lemon Parmesan Aïoli After the basic mayonnaise has been prepared as above, gently whisk in 3 tablespoons freshly grated Parmesan cheese, 1 tablespoon fresh lemon juice, 1 tablespoon mashed garlic (use a mortar and pestle or the side of your knife) and ¾ teaspoon grated lemon zest. Taste for seasoning and adjust. This is much fuller flavored if made and stored in the refrigerator for several hours before using.

Lavender Mayonnaise Prepare the mayonnaise as directed above except in Step 3, add 1 teaspoon minced fresh lavender leaves with the last drizzles of oil. Taste for seasoning and adjust. This is much fuller flavored if made and stored in the refrigerator for several hours before using. Garnish with lavender blossoms or chive blossoms.

Rouille Proceed as above in Step 1. In Step 2, add ½ cup roasted red bell pepper strips, patted dry; 1 small red serrano chile, seeded and chopped; and 1 tablespoon mashed garlic (use a mortar and pestle or the side of your knife). Process until pureed. Replace the safflower oil with 1¼ cups high-quality extra-virgin olive oil. Complete as directed above. Taste for seasoning and adjust. You may want to add a pinch of cayenne or more lemon juice at this point.

Basil Mayonnaise Proceed as above in Step 1. In Step 2, add ⅓ cup shredded basil and puree with other ingredients. One tablespoon minced fresh mint is a great addition, but optional. Thin with a little extra lemon juice, if needed.

Sesame-Ginger Mayonnaise Proceed as above in Step 1. In Step 2, add 3 tablespoons chopped cilantro and process until pureed. In Step 3, replace 3 tablespoons of the oil with toasted sesame oil and complete as directed above. Stir in 1½ tablespoons finely minced or grated ginger. If you are using this on a fish dish, stir in ½ teaspoon fish sauce. Garnish with toasted sesame seeds.

Mustard-Tarragon Mayonnaise Proceed as above in Step 1. In Step 2, add an additional 4 teaspoons Dijon or Meaux (whole grain–type) mustard and 3 tablespoons chopped fresh tarragon and process until pureed. Thin with a little extra vinegar or lemon juice, if needed.

Salsa Rustica

This recipe starts out as a classic table salsa with grilled corn added for crunch. The tomatillo variation is an excellent sauce for a chicken casserole or roasted red snapper in addition to being a good dipping salsa. The shrimp variation is a quick take on ceviche that is particularly festive served on chips topped with melted cheese for a seafood nacho plate.

Makes 1½ cups

1 cup chopped, seeded, peeled fresh tomatoes, juices reserved

2 teaspoons minced jalapeño or serrano chile (1 medium)

¼ cup fresh lime juice

½ cup chopped fresh cilantro or 3 tablespoons chopped fresh oregano

½ cup minced white onion

¼ teaspoon ground cumin

⅛ teaspoon cayenne pepper

½ cup grilled corn kernels (page 60)

1 clove garlic, minced

Pinch sugar

Kosher salt and freshly ground coarse black pepper, to taste

Combine all the ingredients in a medium bowl.

✹ VARIATIONS

Tomatillo Salsa Replace the tomato with 1 cup canned tomatillos. Add 1 teaspoon minced garlic and 1 teaspoon ground cumin. Puree all of the ingredients in a blender except the cilantro. Stir in the cilantro.

Crazy Shrimp Salsa Replace the corn with 1½ cups chopped, cooked shrimp. Replace the cayenne pepper with 4 to 6 dashes hot pepper sauce and increase the garlic to 2 cloves.

A PASSION FOR CHILE PEPPERS

It doesn't matter who you are, or what you've done, or think you can do.
There's a confrontation with destiny awaiting you. Somewhere, there is a
chile you cannot eat.

—Daniel Pinkwater, *A Hot Time in Nairobi*

Spicy food of every kind has become part of the mainstream American diet. We've discovered what people from tropical climates have always known: you get an endorphin rush from a slurp of salsa or a spoonful of sambal. Spicy food also gets a thumbs-up from many health gurus; they say it is good for colds and cholesterol. At any rate, we're hooked. The fire for all of these hot recipes comes from one form or another of chiles: fresh, dried, powdered or pickled, alone or in combination. Chiles are available fresh in the produce section, dried or ground in the spice aisle and sometimes pickled or canned like jalapeños en escabeche and chipotle en adobo. Chiles are often used in combination—one or two types of dried and one fresh—to create complex, sophisticated heat (see the Mole Poblano–Style Chili with Beans, page 103). To use in a recipe, dried chiles can be either soaked in a hot liquid until softened or chopped or ground up and added dry.

Fresh, mild chiles are often used to stuff chiles rellenos and in sauces. Moderate chiles are good in salsa and barbecue sauce. The hottest chiles are used in Asian dishes, stir-fries and chili. The most commonly available cooking chiles (and the ones used in this book), in order of heat from mild to blistering, are:

DRIED CHILES

- Ancho (a dried poblano)
- New Mexico Red

- Guajillo
- Chipotle (smoke-dried jalapeño)
- Pasilla
- Cascabel
- Thai
- De Arbol

FRESH CHILES

- Anaheim
- Poblano
- New Mexico
- Guero (banana, wax pepper)
- Jalapeño (red and green)
- Serrano (red and green)
- De Agua (red and green)
- Thai
- Habanero

CANNED AND PICKLED

- Chipotle en adobo
- Chiles en escabeche

Mango Salsa

This is good on grilled swordfish, shrimp, chicken and cold poached salmon. The Avocado-Chipotle Salsa variation really brightens a pork chop or grilled flank steak.

Makes 2½ cups

1½ cups diced mango or papaya

1 orange, peeled and segmented

1 lemon or lime, peeled and segmented, juice reserved

½ cup minced red onion

4 teaspoons minced serrano chile

½ cup chopped fresh cilantro

½ cup red bell pepper slivers

¼ teaspoon ground cumin

1 teaspoon sugar

1 teaspoon kosher salt

¼ teaspoon white pepper

Combine all the ingredients in a medium bowl.

▓ VARIATION

Avocado-Chipotle Salsa Add 1¼ cups diced ripe avocado (about 2 medium) and ½ to 1 teaspoon minced canned chipotle chiles. Makes about 3½ cups.

COMPOUND BUTTERS

Compound butters are made by softening unsalted butter and mixing it with various spices and aromatics. Chilled compound butters are frequently sliced and placed on hot grilled or broiled meats (see Roast Tenderloin of Beef with Horseradish-Dijon Butter, page 74), poultry or fish, steamed vegetables or hot pasta and allowed to melt. The flavored butter serves as an easy sauce. At other times compound butters are swirled into sauces to finish them.

To make a compound butter, whip unsalted butter until creamy. Then add the flavoring ingredients. Roll the butter mixture into a cylinder about 1 inch thick in a sheet of waxed paper and chill until firm.

Bold mixtures like minced fresh rosemary and crumbled Roquefort can be blended into butter for lamb or beef. A minced chipotle chile and garlic compound butter melts beautifully over broiled pork chops. Grated ginger and minced cilantro butter tastes delicious on fish, and minced tarragon and chervil butter highlights a simple grilled breast of chicken. Minced basil, mint and sun-dried tomatoes or minced mushrooms and garlic make perfect compound butters to serve on top of pasta. The more delicate flavors go best with vegetables and fish and the bolder flavors with lamb, pork and beef.

Fresh lemon or orange juices can also be added to the whipped butter for fish and chicken dishes.

Gorgonzola Cream Sauce

Simple cream reduction sauces are a mainstay of the quick gourmet kitchen. This combination of reduced broth or stock and reduced cream allows you to make a luscious, thick sauce without flour. I serve the Gorgonzola Cream Sauce over grilled filet mignon or any good roast beef. It's also excellent on pasta. The Curry-Coconut Sauce is perfect on oven-roasted fish or chicken. The Cranberry Chèvre variation is exotic on grilled or roasted turkey or chicken; it turns Thanksgiving leftovers into a meal fit for company.

Christy Hedges, who was an invaluable ally in the test kitchen, made this recipe a personal project and delivered tremendous results.

Makes 1¼ cups

4 cups reduced-sodium or unsalted chicken broth

2 tablespoons finely minced shallot

½ cup dry vermouth or white wine

2 tablespoons fresh lemon juice

1 cup whipping cream, heated until hot

1½ teaspoons sugar

2 teaspoons finely minced fresh rosemary

2 teaspoons finely minced fresh thyme

⅓ cup crumbled Gorgonzola or other good-quality creamy blue cheese

Freshly ground coarse black pepper, to taste

1. Boil the chicken broth in a large, wide saucepan over high heat until reduced to 1 cup.
2. Meanwhile, combine the shallot, vermouth and lemon juice in a medium saucepan and bring to a boil. Boil until reduced to a syrupy consistency.
3. Add the reduced broth to the shallot mixture and whisk to combine. Add the hot cream, sugar, rosemary and thyme and simmer briskly for 12 to 15 minutes to blend the flavors and thicken the sauce.
4. Add the Gorgonzola cheese and pepper to taste and whisk to combine. Do not add salt as the cheese will add a salty flavor.

▓ VARIATIONS

Curry-Coconut Sauce In Step 2, instead of the shallot, use 2 tablespoons minced garlic, 1 tablespoon grated fresh ginger and 2 teaspoons minced red jalapeño chile. Replace the vermouth with ½ cup dry sherry and the lemon juice with 1 tablespoon lime juice. Add 1 tablespoon curry powder to the saucepan and reduce. In Step 3, replace the cream with 1 cup coconut milk. Do not use the rosemary or thyme. In Step 4, replace the Gorgonzola cheese with ¼ cup plain full-fat yogurt and 2 tablespoons minced fresh cilantro.

Cranberry Chèvre Sauce In Step 3, replace the herbs with 1 tablespoon finely minced fresh tarragon and add ½ cup minced, dried cranberries. In Step 4, replace the Gorgonzola cheese with ¼ cup mild fresh goat cheese.

CRÈME FRAÎCHE

Crème fraîche is such a tasty addition to your cooking that while it may not be available in every grocery store, it is worth the minimal trouble to make your own.

Heat 1 cup whipping cream to about 98°F (35°C). Stir in 2 tablespoons buttermilk. Cover and store in a glass container in a warm place for 12 to 24 hours or until very thick. At this point the cream can be stirred and refrigerated for up to 1 week.

Because it will not curdle when boiled it is a great addition to thicken sauces or soups. It is also excellent with the addition of a little sugar as a topping for fresh fruit.

Crème fraîche could be used instead of the goat cheese in the Cranberry Chèvre Sauce or in place of the mascarpone in the Fig and Mascarpone Risotto Dolce (page 170).

Ginger Dipping Sauce

Makes about ½ cup

2 tablespoons mirin (sweet rice wine)

3 tablespoons seasoned rice vinegar

1 teaspoon fresh lime juice

⅛ teaspoon Chinese chili oil

2 tablespoons grated fresh ginger

2 tablespoons reduced-sodium soy sauce

2 tablespoons minced fresh cilantro or scallion

1. Mix all the ingredients together.
2. Store for up to 1 week in the refrigerator. Serve on steamed mussels or with crab cakes, dim sum or sushi.

Desserts

AT LARGE, BLACK-TIE WEDDINGS there is always a lot for me to keep an eye on: receiving lines, full glasses for the champagne toast, bandleader-versus-wedding-coordinator negotiations, parental mood swings and, of course, the food. Like any caterer worth their salt, it is my job to smooth out tremors before anyone notices. At one wedding, the guests were surging enthusiastically around the seafood bar as usual and, of course, around the bride and groom. Unfortunately, in violation of every fire code, four hundred exuberant celebrants were wedged into a room designed for three hundred (I had tried to convince them it was too small), along with tables, bars and stemware.

I was adjusting the place cards on the head table when I caught a flicker of action from the corner of my eye. I jerked to attention. As I peered over the tops of dancing heads, it looked as if someone on the other side of the room was moving the five-tier, four-foot-tall wedding cake. For the uninitiated, that is as unwise as serving oysters Rockefeller at a toddler's birthday party.

I couldn't see who had their hands on the table, but whomever it was obviously had no idea what was going to happen next. I shouted to them, "Stop!" But I immediately realized no one could hear me over the band's zealous rendition of "Shake Your Bon Bon." I leapt off the dais and started elbowing my way through the throng, using my clipboard as a polite cattle prod. By the time I broke through to the other side of the room, it was already too late. I arrived just in time to see the groom, an unidentified buddy and the photographer finally heave the very large cake table into the air.

"You need to put that down right now. Carefully." I spoke in the tone you'd use to advise a three year old to let go of a beehive. The groom smiled at me blearily while the photographer assured me he knew what he was doing. "We just need to move the cake over here where the light's better for pictures." As I stepped forward to wrest the table from them, the inevitable happened. The cake shuddered, slid a couple of inches and then fell off the table and into my outstretched arms; simultaneously the band took a break. The bride's mother screamed. Every head in the room turned to see what had caused the ruckus. And the photographer started snapping away.

We eventually scraped the cake off of me and back onto the table, took it into the kitchen and, with the help of our gifted pastry chef, re-created a modest one-layer cake that was good enough for pictures (as long as the light wasn't too good).

When the beaming bride and groom came in the next month to show me their album, I was surprised to see they had included more pictures of the cake disaster than of themselves with the reconstituted cake. In the pictures documenting this moment, it appeared as if I had mischievously thrown myself onto the wedding cake like a cat on a Christmas tree. They giggled while they showed them to me, saying, "It was the coolest part of the reception. Our guests thought we paid you to do that. They were so impressed, we've let them believe we planned it. Thanks for the most memorable wedding cake ceremony ever." I don't imagine this did a lot to enhance my reputation as the cool-as-a-cucumber caterer for all occasions, but that's weddings.

BREW MASTERY

You can make your own perfect cup of coffee by keeping tabs on proportion, grind, water and freshness when you brew.

PROPORTION

The recipe for brewing "the perfect cup" is 2 tablespoons of coffee for each 6 ounces of water. Brewing with too much or too little water will yield an "over-extracted" bitter beverage. Try these proportions and, if necessary, dilute with warm water after brewing.

GRIND

Different brewing methods require different grinds. Be sure your beans are ground precisely for the chosen brewing method (for example, espresso, filter drip, percolator, French press).

WATER

Because a cup of coffee is 98 percent water, the importance of fresh, clean water cannot be stressed enough. Use bottled or filtered water. Start with cold water. If you heat water in a stovetop kettle, bring the water to a boil (212°F [100°C]), remove it from the heat for a few seconds and then pour it over the grinds.

FRESHNESS

Start with freshly roasted, whole bean coffee. Store it away from moisture and air in an airtight container. Grind your coffee just before brewing and, once it's brewed, drink it or hold it in a thermal carafe. Coffee left on a burner begins to decay in 20 minutes and will never recover its fresh taste when reheated.

Black and White Chocolate Terrine

Forget love. . . . I'd rather fall in chocolate.

—Anonymous

Layers of light and dark chocolate ganache are alternated in this dish to create an easy special-occasion dessert that can be finished days ahead of time. Because good-quality chocolate (and you must use the best in this recipe) combines exceptionally well with most liqueurs, nuts and fruits, you can vary this recipe according to what you have on hand or your favorite tastes. I find it's most successful with one layer including something crunchy, like nuts or Almond Roca bits, and the other two layers flavored with complementary spices or liqueurs. The terrine is beautiful served with any of the fresh fruit sauces on page 186, fresh fruit or whipped cream.

Formal • Completed in Advance

PARTY TIME PREPARATIONS: None. This should be finished and in the refrigerator for 4 to 6 hours before the party.

SERVING EQUIPMENT: Individual dessert plates.

BEVERAGE TO ACCOMPANY: Port, Australian Muscat, sweet sherry

Makes 14 to 16 servings

BITTERSWEET LAYER

7 ounces bittersweet chocolate

¾ cup whipping cream

½ teaspoon ground cinnamon

1 teaspoon instant espresso powder

SEMISWEET LAYER

7 ounces semisweet chocolate

⅔ cup whipping cream

2 tablespoons amaretto

WHITE CHOCOLATE LAYER

7 ounces white chocolate

½ cup whipping cream

½ teaspoon ground cinnamon

½ teaspoon freshly grated nutmeg

½ cup pine nuts or almonds, toasted

Fruit sauce of choice (page 186) and whipped cream or fresh fruit, to serve

1. Line an 8 × 4 × 2½-inch loaf pan with aluminum foil smoothed very evenly up all four sides, carefully molding into the corners and letting the foil hang over the edges about 2 inches.

2. **TO MAKE THE BITTERSWEET LAYER:** Roughly chop the chocolate and put it in a food processor. Pulse briefly to finely chop. Be careful not to overprocess and turn the chocolate into a dry paste.

3. Heat the cream, cinnamon and espresso powder in a saucepan over medium heat just to the boiling point. With the motor running, pour the cream into the chocolate and process to melt and blend together completely. Pour the mixture into the lined pan and put in the refrigerator to cool and set.

4. **TO MAKE THE SEMISWEET LAYER:** Roughly chop the semisweet chocolate and put it in the food processor. Pulse briefly to finely chop. Be careful not to overprocess and turn the chocolate into a dry paste.

5. Heat the cream in a saucepan just to the boiling point. With the motor running, pour the cream into the chocolate and process to melt and blend together completely. Add the amaretto and pulse to blend. Pour the mixture into a bowl and refrigerate until thick but still pourable, 2 to 3 hours, stirring several times to make sure that it cools evenly.

6. **TO MAKE THE WHITE CHOCOLATE LAYER:** Roughly chop the white chocolate and put it in the food processor. Pulse briefly to finely chop. Be careful not to overprocess and turn the chocolate into a dry paste.

7. Heat the cream, cinnamon and nutmeg in a saucepan just to the boiling point. With the motor running, pour the cream into the chocolate and process to melt and blend together completely. Pour the mixture into a bowl and refrigerate until thick but still pourable, 2 to 3 hours, stirring several times to make sure that it cools evenly.

8. When the semisweet and white chocolate mixtures are thick, use an electric mixer to whip each of them to a fluffy consistency—like frosting. Fold the nuts into the white chocolate.

9. Check the bittersweet layer in the pan. If it's not firm, pop it into the freezer for 10 minutes before proceeding. When the bottom layer is firm, spread the semisweet chocolate over the chilled bittersweet layer and smooth the top. Cover and freeze for 10 minutes.

10. Remove the pan from the freezer and spread the white chocolate mixture over the top and smooth to an even layer with a spatula. Cover and refrigerate the finished terrine for at least 4 to 6 hours, or overnight, before serving.

11. **TO SERVE:** Use the edges of the foil to unmold the terrine onto a clean cutting board. Peel off the foil and let it sit for 5 to 10 minutes before slicing crosswise into ½-inch-thick slices. Pool one of the fruit sauces on each plate, top with a slice of the terrine and decorate with whipped cream or fresh fruit.

Chocolate à la Mode An option for a dramatic presentation can be created by layering just the two dark chocolate flavors and topping each slice with a tiny scoop of the whipped white chocolate mixture. It looked like a chocolate layer topped with a tiny scoop of vanilla ice cream. To create this, follow the directions above except that the white chocolate goes back into a bowl after being whipped in Step 8.

To serve, cut a slice of the dark loaf and use a melon baller or mini ice cream scoop to create a small truffle of the white chocolate. Set it on the dark wedge and drizzle with one of the fruit sauces on page 186 or garnish with fresh fruit or whipped cream.

Gingered White Chocolate Terrine Replace the cinnamon and nutmeg in Step 7 with ½ teaspoon ground ginger and ⅓ cup minced candied ginger. This is excellent when combined with bittersweet and semisweet layers flavored with coconut extract or grated orange zest.

Candy Bar Blast Terrine Add 3 ounces of roughly chopped Almond Roca candy to the semisweet layer after whipping in Step 8. Delete the pine nuts from the white chocolate layer. Serve with whipped cream and a sprinkle of toasted sliced almonds.

CHOCOLATE 101

The Latin describing the seed of the cocoa tree translates to "food of the gods." Judging by dessert menus in all the best restaurants, Americans concur. There are many types of chocolate used in cooking. In order of percentage of chocolate liquor, and therefore intensity of chocolate flavor, they are unsweetened, bittersweet, semisweet (slightly more sugar than bittersweet), sweet and milk chocolate (which also contains 12 percent milk). White chocolate is technically not a chocolate because it does not contain chocolate liquor, but it does contain 20 percent cocoa butter and is commonly thought of as a type of chocolate.

When selecting chocolate, look for one that contains 31 to 40 percent cocoa butter (the fat that is pressed out of chocolate liquor when cocoa is processed). In some less expensive brands of chocolate some of the cocoa butter may be replaced by another fat. This affects the flavor and eating quality of the chocolate.

Because chocolate is often melted before use in recipes, it's important to know how to melt it successfully. There are two imperatives: do not allow any trace of water or steam to come in contact with the chocolate and never overheat the chocolate as it will become grainy instead of smooth. An easy way to melt chocolate is in the microwave. Chop the chocolate into ½-inch pieces and place in a microwave-safe bowl. Microwave uncovered at medium power. Stir with a rubber spatula after 30 seconds. Continue to heat and stir at 30-second intervals until the chocolate is melted. Do not try to microwave more than 8 ounces at a time.

Some particularly reliable brands of chocolate for cooking include Scharffen Berger, Valrhona, Schokinag and Ghirardelli. Buying chocolate in large bars is the best buy, but remember it ideally should be stored in an airtight container between 60 and 70°F (15 to 20°C), away from direct sunlight.

Crème Brûlée

Without butter, without eggs, there is no reason to come to France.

—Paul Bocuse

A crunchy top that you must shatter to reach the silky custard beneath creates the sexy juxtaposition of textures, which have made crème brûlée one of America's most popular desserts. There are many variations on this simple custard. I have included three classics: vanilla, espresso and Mexican chocolate, each with a little surprise in the crust. You can add a tablespoon of finely sliced ripe fruit like raspberry, peach or mango in the bottom of each ramekin to add flair to any of the flavors.

Formal • Completed in Advance

PARTY TIME PREPARATIONS: None. This should be finished and in the refrigerator at least 1 hour before the party.

SERVING EQUIPMENT: You will serve the crèmes in the individual ramekins in which they were baked.

BEVERAGE TO ACCOMPANY: Champagne, Vin Santo, cognac

Makes 8 servings

CRÈME
1 teaspoon unsalted butter
1 cup slivered ripe fruit or small berries (optional)
4 eggs
3 egg yolks
1 cup heavy whipping cream
1 cup milk

2 tablespoons amaretto or frangelico
⅓ cup sugar
1 teaspoon pure vanilla extract
Pinch salt

TOPPING
½ cup sugar
1 tablespoon plus 1 teaspoon finely grated orange zest

1. Preheat the oven to 300°F (150°C). Lightly brush 8 (3-inch) ramekins with melted butter and place in a large roasting pan. (If using fruit, divide the fruit evenly among the ramekins.)
2. Whisk eggs and egg yolks until slightly thickened. When well blended, stir in the cream, milk, liqueur, sugar, vanilla and salt. Pour this mixture into the prepared ramekins.
3. Carefully pour enough hot water into the baking pan to reach halfway up the sides of the ramekins. Bake about 30 minutes, until barely set when you gently jiggle them. It will still look runny in the middle.

4. Remove the pan from the oven and let cool. When cool, remove the ramekins from the pan, tightly cover each ramekin with plastic wrap and refrigerate at least 2 hours or up to 2 days. The custard will remain slightly soft in the center, even when cool.

5. **TO FINISH:** Preheat broiler and place a rack as close to the flame as possible.

6. **FOR THE TOPPING:** Use a fork to toss the sugar lightly with the orange zest. Sprinkle an even layer of the sugar mixture across each custard to cover completely, about 1 tablespoon each.

7. Place the sugared ramekins on a baking sheet and place under the broiler until the sugar caramelizes (colors) and bubbles, 2 to 4 minutes. Depending on your broiler, you may need to rotate them with tongs to color evenly. Remove and let cool. The sugar top will harden. The crèmes may be served immediately. However, I prefer them chilled for at least one hour. (Note: If refrigerated for more than 3 hours the sugar crust will begin to weep.)

❧ VARIATIONS

Espresso Crème Brûlée with a Twist of Lemon Heat the combined cream and milk in the microwave to hot, about 1½ minutes. If necessary, continue to heat in 30-second increments, stopping to test so as not to boil the milk. Into the hot milk, whisk 3 tablespoons instant espresso powder, 1½ teaspoons unsweetened cocoa powder and ½ teaspoon freshly ground black pepper.

When this liquid mixture has cooled to room temperature, continue with the main recipe instructions at Step 2. Replace the orange zest in Step 6 with 1 tablespoon plus 1 teaspoon finely grated lemon zest.

Mexican Chocolate Crème Brûlée Heat the combined cream and milk in the microwave to hot, about 1½ minutes. If necessary, continue to heat in 30-second increments. To the hot milk, add 4 ounces chopped milk chocolate, ¼ cup unsweetened cocoa powder, ¾ teaspoon espresso powder and ¾ teaspoon ground cinnamon. Whisk until the chocolate is completely melted into the liquid. You may need to heat for an additional 30 to 45 seconds to encourage the chocolate to melt. When this liquid mixture has cooled to room temperature, continue with the main recipe instructions at Step 2. To enhance the chocolate, reduce the vanilla extract to ½ teaspoon and replace the amaretto with 2 tablespoons Kahlúa. Finish as above.

WHEN TO SERVE CHAMPAGNE

Come quickly, I am tasting the stars!
—Dom Perignon, at the moment he discovered champagne

For many, the question of when to serve champagne is really a question of when *not* to serve it. Champagne does seem to go with everything, from brunch to dessert and everything in between, including those intervals before or between courses when conversations bloom. And with only a few exceptions, I find myself largely in agreement on this point. Still, champagne service traditionally comes at the very beginning of an event, as guests arrive and coats are checked. People often take their glass of champagne to the table for a toast to begin their meal as well. If you want to experiment with food matches, I recommend sticking with mild flavors; white fish, shrimp, poached chicken, cream sauces, simple salads and lightly fried dishes work well with champagnes, while more richly seasoned dishes and spicy foods tend to overwhelm the delicate flavors of the wine and even make it taste a bit bitter. As for desserts, champagne works best with simple, light selections like biscotti or fruit tarts, while very rich or sweet desserts will definitely make your bubbles go bitter.

Dessert Crepes

Crepes can be filled and baked, rolled and fried or used as the foundation for a good fruit or chocolate sauce. This recipe can be varied to include vanilla, ground cinnamon or ginger in the batter. If you don't have a special crepe pan, a good omelet pan will do. The pan should have a 5- to 6-inch wide bottom with sloping sides.

One of my favorite ways to serve these crepes is to simply fold them into quarters, drizzle on a little butter and warm them in the oven. When they are hot, sprinkle on a combination of sliced strawberries tossed with finely shredded basil, sugar and cinnamon. Strawberries and basil are magical together.

Formal • Buffet

PARTY TIME PREPARATIONS: Heat and serve.

SERVING EQUIPMENT: For a buffet, chafing dishes or hot tray. Individual dessert plates and pie server or large spoon.

Makes 16 to 20 (6-inch) crepes

CREPES
1 cup all-purpose flour
1 tablespoon sugar
1/2 teaspoon salt
1/2 cup water
1/2 cup plus 1 tablespoon milk
2 eggs
2 tablespoons butter, melted
3 tablespoons frangelico

4 teaspoons grated lemon zest
Vegetable oil, for cooking

TO SERVE
Filling (see below)
3 tablespoons unsalted butter, melted
Powdered sugar
Berries, shaved chocolate, whipped cream or ice cream

1. Combine the flour, sugar and salt in a bowl.
2. Place all liquid ingredients in a blender and pulse to mix. With the motor running, pour in the flour mixture. Scrape down the sides and blend again to thoroughly mix, about 20 seconds. The batter should be about the consistency of heavy cream. Stir in the zest. Cover and chill for at least 1 hour before using (or up to 24 hours).
3. Pour a small amount of vegetable oil into the crepe pan and wipe out with a paper towel. You will not have to grease the pan again.
4. Place the pan over medium heat. When the pan is hot, add 2 to 3 tablespoons of the chilled batter. Lifting the pan off the burner, swirl the batter around the pan to

form an even, very thin coating. The first side will be golden in about 1 minute. Loosen lightly with the edge of a spatula, flip and cook the second side for about 1 minute. Don't worry if the first couple don't turn out. That seems to happen to everyone as you become used to the temperature of the pan and just how to swivel your wrist to swirl the batter. I usually count on throwing the first few out.

5. Transfer each completed crepe to a rack to cool and proceed with the next. If you are making the crepes for future use, layer the cooled crepes with waxed paper and freeze or refrigerate.

6. **TO FILL:** Spread 1 rounded tablespoon of filling across the middle of the crepe and fold in half and then into quarters. Put in a buttered baking dish, overlapping the fans as you go. Crepes can be prepared to this stage, well wrapped and refrigerated up to 24 hours in advance.

7. **TO BAKE:** Preheat the oven to 400°F (205°C). Drizzle folded crepes with melted butter. Bake for 10 to 12 minutes, until bubbling. Serve two or three crepe fans per person dusted with powdered sugar and garnished as desired.

⁂ FILLINGS

Cinnamon-Apple Filling

1 cup (2 sticks) unsalted butter, softened	3 tablespoons frangelico
3 cups thinly sliced apples, ripe apricots or small, whole blueberries	1½ teaspoons ground cinnamon
6 tablespoons light brown sugar	1 tablespoon fresh lemon juice
6 tablespoons clover honey	

Heat 3 tablespoons of the butter in a large sauté pan over medium heat. When bubbling, add the fruit and sauté 4 to 6 minutes, until softened. Stir in all remaining ingredients and set aside to cool on the counter or in the refrigerator. When cool proceed with filling directions in Step 6.

In Step 7, top with ¼ cup toasted, sliced almonds before drizzling with butter.

Ginger-Orange Filling

1 cup unsalted butter

2 cups thinly sliced mango or minced kiwi or raspberries

¾ cup sugar

3 tablespoons grated orange zest

2 tablespoons orange juice

4 teaspoons grated fresh ginger

Heat 2 tablespoons of the butter in a large sauté pan over medium heat. When bubbling, add the fruit and sauté 2 to 3 minutes, until softened. Stir in all remaining ingredients and set aside to cool on the countertop or in the refrigerator. When cool proceed with filling directions in Step 6. Top with Grand Marnier–flavored whipped cream or coconut ice cream.

Nutella Filling Combine 1 (13-ounce) jar Nutella chocolate hazelnut spread and ½ cup chopped, toasted almonds or hazelnuts. Proceed with filling and baking instructions. Serve topped with coffee ice cream or whipped cream flavored with brandy.

Lemon Amaretto Cheesecake

Nearly everyone's short list of dessert favorites includes cheesecake. It's luscious, light and decadent all at the same time. And for the home cook, it offers remarkable scope for creativity. This basic recipe, including the unexpected lushness of chèvre, can be the basis for many, many more variations than the ones included here.

Quick and Easy • Buffet • Formal

PARTY TIME PREPARATIONS: None. This should be finished and in the refrigerator at least 3 hours before the party.

SERVING EQUIPMENT: If on a buffet, a flat serving platter, serrated knife and pie server.

BEVERAGE TO ACCOMPANY: Vin Santo, sweet sherry

Makes 12 servings

NUT CRUST

5 tablespoons unsalted butter, melted

4 ounces graham crackers (makes about 1 cup crumbs)

¾ cup almonds (makes about ¾ cup ground)

5 tablespoons light brown sugar

FILLING

1½ pounds cream cheese, room temperature

12 ounces mild, fresh chèvre, room temperature

1 cup sugar

4 large eggs

Grated zest and juice from 2 lemons

3 tablespoons amaretto

2 teaspoons pure vanilla extract

½ cup sliced almonds, toasted

Raspberry Sauce (page 186)

1. Preheat the oven to 325°F (165°C). Use 1 tablespoon of the butter to coat a 3-inch deep, 9-inch-round springform pan. Combine the graham crackers, nuts and sugar in a food processor and process until finely ground. Add remaining melted butter and pulse to mix. The crust will look somewhat dry and crumbly. Press the crust into the pan, covering the bottom and 2 inches up the side. Use heavy aluminum foil to wrap around the exterior bottom of the pan and at least 1 inch up the side to keep water out. Chill while you assemble the filling.

2. Have all of your filling ingredients at room temperature. With your electric mixer set on low, use the paddle to combine the cream cheese and chèvre just until smooth. Add the sugar and blend briefly. Add the eggs, one at a time, mixing as briefly as possible to incorporate each egg. Blend in all remaining ingredients, except the almonds and sauce.

3. Pour the filling into the chilled crust. Put the wrapped pan on a shallow baking pan or jelly roll pan and add enough hot water to cover to a depth of ½ inch. Bake for 40 minutes then sprinkle on the almonds and cook another 15 minutes. The cheesecake will appear barely set, still jiggly in the middle; take it out anyway.

4. Put the cheesecake pan directly on a cooling rack. When cool, wrap well and refrigerate. The cheesecake should be refrigerated at least 3 hours before serving; overnight is even better.

5. **TO SERVE:** Loosen the sides of the springform pan and remove. Use a serrated knife to slice through the cheesecake. The center will remain quite soft and the texture throughout is tender and delicate. Lay each piece on its side and drizzle luxuriously with raspberry sauce.

VARIATIONS

Nectarine Amaretto Cheesecake Cover ½ cup chopped dried nectarines or apricots with 3 tablespoons amaretto and 1 tablespoon water. Cover lightly in plastic wrap and heat in the microwave on High for 60 seconds. Set aside to cool, then puree the nectarines and the liquid and the lemon juice in a blender or mini processor.

Assemble the original filling recipe minus the amaretto (it's in with the nectarines). Decrease the vanilla extract to 1 teaspoon. Add the nectarine puree into the filling mixture along with ½ teaspoon almond extract and 1 teaspoon ground ginger. Proceed as above.

White Chocolate–Banana-Coconut Cheesecake For the crust, use the Ginger Snap Crust (page 167). Line pan and chill as directed above.

To create the exotic banana-tinged filling, add 4 ounces melted white chocolate, 1 cup mashed ripe banana and 1 teaspoon ground nutmeg to the filling and replace the frangelico with 2 tablespoons rum. Proceed as above.

WINE WITH DESSERT

It's often a matter of wine *with* dessert or wine *as* dessert. If the answer is the latter, any number of rich, sweet wines are wonderful on their own. Ports and Sauternes are the most famous, of course, though not the only choices. If it's a matter of matching a wine to desserts, however, it's best to focus on the flavors in the dessert and to find a wine that doesn't cover them up, but adds nuances of its own. When pairing wine with desserts there is one basic to keep in mind: the level of sugar in the wine must be greater than the sweetness of the dessert. If the wine has less sweetness by comparison, it will taste sour alongside your dessert. For fruit-based treats, I favor Sauternes, late-harvest Rieslings or Chenin Blancs, whose inherent stone fruit characteristics complement these types of desserts beautifully. Vanilla and chocolate creations call for wines with robust red fruit flavors like ports, Australian Muscats or sweet sherries, which serve almost as sauces. Cookies and other pastry-type desserts are great with elegant and restrained wines like Sauternes and Italian Vin Santo, while very cold items, ice creams, glaces, custards and the like almost always fight with dessert wines. In these situations, it's best to serve the dessert and then a glass of something scrumptious afterward to accompany the cordial conversations among your guests.

Lemon Tart

A lemon tart appears on everyone's top-ten dessert list. It is beautiful all on its own or garnished with summer fruit or a dollop of whipped cream. These three variations explore some of the most enticing flavors to combine with lemon: white chocolate, blueberry and ginger. The simple and forgiving Coconut Ginger Snap Crust, a contribution from my masseuse Tiffany Atkinson, is a great addition to your dessert repertoire. It can be used to enhance any simple fruit tart, cheesecake, mousse pie or ice cream pie.

A lovely variation on the basic lemon tart is also created by using half lemon juice and half lime juice.

Formal • Buffet • Completed in Advance

PARTY TIME PREPARATIONS: None. This should be finished and in the refrigerator before the party.

SERVING EQUIPMENT: If on a buffet, a flat serving platter and pie server.

BEVERAGE TO ACCOMPANY: Vin Santo, sweet sherry

Makes 10 servings; 11-inch tart

GINGER SNAP CRUST

1 cup plus 6 tablespoons lightly packed sweetened flaked coconut

8 tablespoons unsalted butter

1½ cups finely ground ginger snap crumbs (ground in the food processor)

FILLING

1½ cups sugar

1 cup fresh lemon juice

3 eggs

6 egg yolks, lightly beaten

2 tablespoons grated lemon zest

Pinch salt

¾ cup cold unsalted butter, cut in small pieces

2 teaspoons frangelico

Powdered sugar and blueberries, to serve

1. **TO MAKE THE CRUST:** Preheat the oven to 325°F (165°C). Spread the coconut onto a baking sheet and bake until golden brown, about 10 minutes, stirring occasionally. Cool before using.

2. Melt the butter in a saucepan over low heat; cool to tepid. Finely crush the coconut with your hands and add it to the butter along with the crumbs. Blend with a fork.

3. Press evenly into the bottom and sides of an 11-inch tart pan (if you have a second pan about the same size you can set it on top of the crust and use it to press a perfect shell). Bake 20 minutes, until golden brown. Let cool.

4. **TO MAKE THE FILLING:** Dissolve the sugar in the lemon juice in a large, nonreactive bowl or the top half of a double boiler. Whisk in the eggs, egg yolks, lemon zest and salt.

5. Place the bowl with the egg mixture over a pan of gently boiling water. The bowl should fit snugly into the pan without touching the water. Cook over low heat, stirring with a wooden spoon or spatula, for 12 to 14 minutes, until the mixture becomes thick enough to coat the back of a spoon.

6. Remove from the heat and stir to cool slightly. Add the butter, a piece at a time, stirring until completely incorporated. Add the frangelico. Pour the filling into the prebaked crust. Chill until set, for at least 3 hours and up to 1 day. Serve with a dusting of powdered sugar and fresh berries.

✺ VARIATIONS

Blueberry-Lemon Tart In Step 6, replace the frangelico with amaretto. Pour ⅔ of the finished, warm lemon mixture into the shell (refrigerate the rest to spread on muffins or serve on ice cream). Let it set up for 10 to 15 minutes, then sprinkle on 2½ cups washed, well-dried fresh blueberries or pitted sweet cherries and gently press into place. Chill until set, for at least 3 hours or overnight. Serve with whipped cream to which you've added powdered sugar and a generous pinch of cinnamon.

White Chocolate–Lemon Cloud Coarsely chop 4 to 5 ounces of good-quality white chocolate. Complete the recipe as above and pour the warm curd into the prepared shell. Sprinkle the white chocolate over the surface and let it set for a minute to begin to melt. Using a knife, draw feathery patterns of the melting white chocolate through the lemon, leaving some chunks. You will have a lovely marbled yellow and white cloud pattern. Chill until set, for at least 3 hours or overnight. If berries are in season, serve each slice with raspberries or strawberry slices.

Orange–Ginger Tart Replace ⅓ of the lemon juice with fresh orange juice. Add 2 teaspoons minced or grated fresh ginger into the mixture in Step 1. Complete as directed.

> NOTE: Any extra lemon curd can be refrigerated for up to 1 week. Use as a cake filling, to line a fruit tart or to make tartlets.

Risotto Dolce Scented with Cardamom and Orange

I consider the discovery of a dish which sustains our appetite and prolongs our pleasures as a far more interesting event than the discovery of a star.
—Henrion de Pensey

I got the idea for a risotto-style dessert from a friend, and Christy Hedges, one of my test kitchen superstars, ran with the idea. We were all intrigued by the concept of using the short, creamy Arborio rice for a pudding. Christy's resulting recipes more than rewarded our expectations. Rice pudding is generally categorized as an informal, homestyle dessert. But with the addition of exotic spices and creative presentations, these silky, risotto-style puddings will complement any formal dinner party. Served on beautiful china or crystal plates with a glass of dessert wine, Risotto Dolce is elegant and impressive, yet quick and easy to make.

Formal • Quick and Easy

PARTY TIME PREPARATIONS: **Assemble and broil.**

SERVING EQUIPMENT: **Individual dessert plates and spoons.**

BEVERAGE TO ACCOMPANY: **Late harvest Riesling, Sauterne, Dry Sack Sherry**

Makes 8 servings

1 cup sugar

5 cups whole milk

1 vanilla bean or 1½ teaspoons vanilla extract

1 teaspoon ground cardamom

¼ teaspoon salt

1 cup Arborio (short grain) rice

1 teaspoon orange flower water (if unavailable, this can be omitted)

1 tablespoon Grand Marnier or Cointreau

4 large smooth-skinned oranges

4 tablespoons slivered blanched almonds, toasted (see note, page 138)

1½ tablespoons grated orange zest, being careful to avoid the bitter white pith, plus extra for garnish

¼ teaspoon freshly grated nutmeg

1. Put ½ cup of the sugar, milk, vanilla bean (split in half with insides scraped into pot), cardamom and salt in a heavy 5-quart saucepan. Bring to a boil, stirring continuously. Add the rice. Boil for 1 minute and reduce the heat to medium. Simmer

until tender but not mushy, about 30 minutes, making sure the milk does not boil over; stir frequently to keep the rice from sticking.

2. Remove the vanilla bean. Stir in the orange flower water and Grand Marnier. Remove from the heat and allow to cool. (Steps 1 and 2 can be made up to 2 days ahead and stored in the refrigerator.)

3. Slice the oranges in half and hollow out the insides. Trim the bases so they stand firmly. Mix the rice pudding with the almonds and orange zest. Fill the orange shells with the rice pudding.

4. Mix the remaining sugar and the nutmeg together and sprinkle on top of each serving. Place the filled orange halves on a baking sheet under a hot broiler for about 5 minutes or until golden brown. This time may vary so it is best to keep checking. Allow to cool slightly before serving to allow the sugar glaze to harden. Garnish with a sprinkle of orange zest.

✹ VARIATIONS

Coconut-Ginger Risotto Dolce Instead of the milk in Step 1, use 2 (14-ounce) cans coconut milk and 1¾ cups whole milk. Omit the cardamom. Take care when simmering the coconut milk mixture that it does not scorch. It should be stirred occasionally. Check for doneness at 25 minutes. In Step 2, omit the orange flower water and substitute 1 tablespoon coconut rum for the Grand Marnier. In Step 3, you may use 4-ounce ramekins or small fresh green coconuts if available. Mix the pudding with 4 tablespoons chopped crystallized ginger and 1 tablespoon grated lime zest. In Step 4, omit the nutmeg and sprinkle the filled ramekins or coconut halves with the regular sugar. Place the ramekins or coconuts on a baking sheet under a hot broiler for about 5 minutes or until golden brown. This time may vary so it is best to keep checking. Cool slightly. Garnish with a sprinkle of lime zest.

Fig and Mascarpone Risotto Dolce Follow Steps 1 and 2. In Step 3, mix the rice pudding with ½ cup mascarpone cheese (crème fraîche could also be used), 4 tablespoons chopped raw pistachios and 2 tablespoons Marsala. Omit the almonds and orange zest. Prepare 16 fresh figs (Black Mission are particularly nice) by trimming the bases of the figs so they stand firmly. Cut an X in the top of each fig and continue cutting about halfway down the sides. Gently fold the "petals" partially open and fill the centers with ¼ cup rice pudding. In Step 4, omit the nutmeg and sprinkle with regular sugar. Place under a hot broiler in a flameproof baking dish (they should be slightly crowded in the dish since the figs have a tendency to open up while cooking) for about 5 minutes or until golden brown. This time may vary so it is best to keep checking. Allow to cool. Garnish with a sprinkle of chopped pistachios.

Rustic Apple-Cranberry Tart

In this recipe, a bottom and top layer of crisply sugared puff pastry create a dramatic, free-form fruit tart. The rustic appearance of this fruit dessert is its visual appeal and its hostess appeal. The crust is roughly rolled out, pinched up over great fruit flavors and baked. This simple preparation is made even easier by using purchased puff pastry. You can whip dessert together in 10 minutes.

This tart is best baked and served, not reheated. This isn't a problem because it can be assembled and refrigerated for up to 1 day before baking. All of the variations are great served with good ice cream or a dollop of barely sweetened whipped cream.

Casual • Picnic • Kid Appeal

PARTY TIME PREPARATIONS: Bake and serve.

SERVING EQUIPMENT: A 12- to 14-inch flat platter, pie server or spatula.

BEVERAGE TO ACCOMPANY: Champagne, late harvest Riesling

Makes 8 generous servings

1 (17-ounce) package frozen puff pastry, thawed in the refrigerator

3 to 4 tart Granny Smith apples (4 cups), peeled, cored and thinly sliced

¾ cup dried cranberries or dried tart cherries

1 tablespoon fresh lemon juice

½ tablespoon grated lemon zest

2 tablespoons cornstarch

¼ cup sugar, or more, depending on fruit, plus 3 to 4 tablespoons, for sprinkling

¼ cup packed light brown sugar

¼ teaspoon freshly grated nutmeg

1 teaspoon ground cinnamon

¼ teaspoon kosher salt

1 egg, lightly beaten

2 tablespoons cold butter, cut into pieces

1. Roll both sheets of the pastry out on a lightly floured board and cut into 12-inch circles. Keep the trimmings to decorate the assembled tart.

2. Line a jelly roll pan with parchment paper and sprinkle with a light dusting of cornmeal. Place 1 sheet of pastry on the parchment. Cover with plastic wrap or parchment and lay on the second sheet. Cover and refrigerate the pastry while you prepare the filling ingredients.

3. Take the pastry out of the refrigerator and remove the top layer from the stack, leaving the bottom one on the sheet pan. Toss the sliced apples, dried cranberries and remaining ingredients, except for the butter, in a large bowl to mix completely.

Pile the filling in the center of the bottom sheet of pastry, being sure to leave a 2-inch border around the edge of the pastry. Brush the border with the beaten egg. Dot the top of the fruit with the butter pieces.

4. Lay the second circle of pastry over the filling to cover completely and touch the bottom sheet. Fold the moistened edge of the bottom pastry over the top edge. Brush the new edge with egg and roll over again, pressing to seal. Using the back of a fork, work around the edge rolling the tines up and over the folded border, pressing firmly to really seal the fruit in. Cut strips, twist ropes or make leaves or stars from the leftover pastry. Brush on one side with cold water and press into place on the top of the tart.

5. Chill the assembled pastry for 40 minutes. The tart can be prepared up to this stage, tightly wrapped and held in the refrigerator for up to 24 hours before baking.

6. Preheat oven to 425°F (220°C). Cut 3 or 4 slits in the top crust to allow hot air to escape during baking. Brush the top lightly with water or milk, and sprinkle generously with 3 to 4 tablespoons sugar. Bake for 30 to 35 minutes, until golden brown and crispy. You may need to loosely set a piece of aluminum foil on top of the tart if it begins to brown too much in the last few minutes of baking. Allow to cool for 10 to 20 minutes before slicing to serve.

▦ VARIATIONS

Rustic Plum-Blackberry Tart Replace the sliced apples and cranberries with 4 cups sliced, firm ripe plums (about 1½ pounds) and ½ cup blackberries. (If you use frozen berries, make sure they are packed without sugar and thaw and drain very well before using.)

Increase the cornstarch you toss with the fruit to 2½ tablespoons. Replace the lemon zest with 1 tablespoon orange zest, replace the cinnamon with 1 teaspoon ground ginger and use ⅓ to ½ cup granulated sugar and no brown sugar. Finish as for apples.

Rustic Pear-Ginger Tart Replace the apples and dried cranberries with 4½ cups peeled, sliced Bartlett, Bosc or Anjou pears (about 4). Eliminate the ¼ cup of brown sugar and replace the cinnamon with 1 teaspoon ground candied ginger (or dry ground ginger). Finish as for apples.

THE FROZEN FRUIT SOLUTION

No one, no matter where they happen to live, can get fresh fruit year round. Of course this does not stop us from wanting a peach and berry cobbler in the dead of winter. In the past we had two options: use fruit that was canned in syrup or delay our gratification until summer. Those days are over. Today you can find several high-quality, frozen fruit brands in your grocer's freezer. Picked, processed and packaged to be as versatile and flavorful as fresh when used in sauces and fillings (no sugar or preservatives added in most cases), these frozen fruit products are an excellent alternative to fresh. In addition to the assortment of berries (including raspberries, strawberries, blackberries, loganberries and blueberries), you can find fresh frozen cherries, peaches, mangos, apples, pears and plums. For top-quality organic fruit look for Cascadian Farm.

Celebration Cakes

When we started experimenting with creating celebration cakes based on the time-saving step of beginning with a cake mix, I was astonished at the results. I hadn't been sure that we could come up with cakes that I felt would really be worthy of your special cake occasions: birthdays, weddings and anniversaries. But I was wrong. These cakes are all full-flavored, moist and elegant.

Each of the following cakes presents a simple stir-and-bake variation to purchased white and devil's food cake mixes. There are several brands in most grocery stores; they are interchangeable for the purposes of these recipes. Most of the cakes can be made as layer cakes, Bundt cakes, loaf cakes or cupcakes.

The Great White Cakes

The following recipes all start with 1 box of white cake mix. The delicate orange blossom cake, suitable for a wedding shower, tea party or anniversary floats on a cloud of delicate orange blossom aroma. Almonds and sherry are blended in the Almond-Amontillado Cake to create a delicate, subtle cake suitable for any occasion. The Coconut-Macadamia Cake is a showstopper. A great coconut cake is always a favorite, especially with men, and this cake certainly qualifies.

Quick and Easy • Completed in Advance • Kid Appeal

PARTY TIME PREPARATIONS: None.

SERVING EQUIPMENT: A 12- to 14-inch flat platter, pie server or spatula.

BEVERAGE TO ACCOMPANY: Champagne, Vin Santo, cognac

Sharon's Orange Blossom Cake

I think this is best with the Dark Chocolate Ganache (page 187). Fresh sliced peaches or berries are great to place in a mound in the center if baked in a Bundt pan.

Makes 2 (9-inch) layers or 1 Bundt cake

1 box white cake mix	2 teaspoons Grand Marnier or triple sec
1¼ cups buttermilk	2 teaspoons orange flower water
½ cup unsalted butter, melted	2 teaspoons orange extract or grated orange zest
3 large eggs	
2 teaspoons vanilla extract	

1. Preheat the oven to 350°F (180°C). Butter the interior of your cake pans; if using rounds, cover the bottoms with a circle of buttered waxed or parchment paper. Sprinkle flour over the entire inside of the greased pans and turn over to shake out any extra flour.

2. Combine all ingredients in the bowl of your mixer and mix for 30 seconds. Scrape down the bowl and beaters and blend for no more than 2 minutes longer. Pour into prepared pan(s).

3. Bake 9-inch layers for 30 minutes or until a toothpick inserted in the centers comes out clean. Bake the Bundt cake for about 50 minutes.

4. Let rest in the pan(s) about 5 minutes before inverting onto a cake rack to cool. Let cool completely before frosting.

Coconut-Macadamia Cake

To create a stunning layer cake, use the Rum Butter Cream Frosting (page 189) and press 2 cups toasted coconut into the sides of the finished cake.

Makes 2 (9-inch) layer cakes or 1 Bundt cake

1 box white cake mix

¾ cup sour cream

½ cup Coco Lopez cream of coconut

½ cup unsalted butter, melted

3 eggs

1 cup shredded, sweetened moist coconut

2 teaspoons vanilla extract

¼ cup dark rum

1 cup coarsely chopped, unsalted macadamia nuts

½ teaspoon freshly grated nutmeg

½ teaspoon ground ginger

1. Heat oven, prepare pans and mix as in Steps 1 and 2 above.
2. Bake 9-inch layers for 30 minutes or until a toothpick inserted in the centers comes out clean. Bake the Bundt cake for about 50 minutes.
3. Let rest in the pan(s) about 5 minutes before inverting onto a cake rack to cool. Let cool completely before frosting.

Almond-Amontillado Cake

There is an extra step required for this cake in order to blend the almond paste with the other ingredients. Frost with the Dark Chocolate Ganache (page 187).

Makes 2 (9-inch) layer cakes or 1 Bundt cake

¾ cup almond paste

3 large eggs

¼ cup vegetable shortening

1 box white cake mix

¾ cup Amontillado or other medium-sweet sherry

2 tablespoons amaretto

¼ cup orange juice

1 teaspoon vanilla extract

¼ cup sour cream

1 teaspoon baking powder

½ teaspoon nutmeg

½ teaspoon cinnamon or mace

1. Use an electric mixer to whip the almond paste and the eggs until blended. Add the shortening and beat to mix. Add all remaining ingredients and mix until fluffy, no more than 5 minutes.
2. Preheat the oven to 350°F (180°C). Bake 9-inch layers for 40 to 45 minutes or until

a toothpick inserted in the centers comes out clean. Bake the Bundt cake for about 60 minutes.

3. Let rest in the pan(s) about 5 minutes before inverting onto a cake rack to cool. Let cool completely before frosting.

The Devil Made Me Do It

Each of the following cakes begins with one package of devil's food cake mix. In order to achieve really memorable flavors, we enhanced the chocolatey richness of the mix in three classic variations. Two types of chocolate were added to the Chocolate-Cognac Cake to create an almost fudgy flavor that appeals to the chocolate lovers in every crowd. The addition of a poached whole orange introduces a very sophisticated flavor and aroma into the Chocolate-Orange Cake, making it suitable for any grown-up affair. The Mexican Chocolate Cake presents an exotic, indulgent flavor that is still intensely chocolate. This combination is enhanced by the Kahlúa-flavored frosting.

All of the basic instructions are the same for the chocolate cakes as for white cakes except how to test for doneness. It is more successful to test a chocolate cake by pressing it gently on the sides and in the middle. When it springs back, it's done. The toothpick test is not as successful on these dark cakes.

Chocolate-Cognac Cake

This elegant, special-occasion cake is best topped with the Dark Chocolate Ganache (page 187) to create a quadruple chocolate treat.

Makes two (9-inch) layer cakes or one Bundt cake.

1 box devil's food cake mix	3 eggs
2 tablespoons unsweetened cocoa powder	⅓ cup vegetable oil
½ cup grated bittersweet chocolate	1 cup chopped walnuts
¼ cup cognac	1 cup milk

1. Preheat the oven to 350°F (180°C). Butter the interior of your cake pans; if using rounds, cover the bottoms with a circle of waxed or parchment paper and butter these also. Sprinkle flour over the entire inside of the greased pans and turn over to shake out any extra flour.

2. Combine all ingredients in the bowl of your mixer and mix for 30 seconds. Scrape down the bowl and beaters and blend for no more than 2 minutes longer. Pour into prepared pan(s).

3. Bake 9-inch layers for 20 to 22 minutes or until they spring back when pressed on the sides and in the middle. Bake the Bundt cake for about 40 minutes.

4. Let rest in the pan(s) about 5 minutes before inverting onto a cake rack to cool. Let cool completely before frosting.

Chocolate-Orange Cake

This looks (and tastes) beautiful frosted with the White Chocolate–Ginger Ganache (page 188).

1 orange	4 eggs
1 box devil's food cake mix	⅓ cup vegetable shortening
2 tablespoons unsweetened cocoa powder	¼ cup triple sec
½ cup grated bittersweet chocolate	¼ cup orange marmalade
2 tablespoons cognac	¾ teaspoon baking soda

1. Put the whole orange in a saucepan and cover with water. Bring to a gentle boil and simmer about 1 hour, until the orange feels quite soft. Remove from the water, let cool, then puree in a food processor. Measure out 1 cup puree. Mix as in Step 2 above, adding the orange puree.
2. Bake 9-inch layers for 45 to 50 minutes at 350°F (180°C), until they spring back when pressed on the sides and in the middle. Bake the Bundt cake for about 60 minutes.
3. Let rest in the pan(s) about 5 minutes before inverting onto a cake rack to cool. Let cool completely before frosting.

Mexican Chocolate Cake

This is very elegant served with the Coffee Butter Cream Frosting (page 189). For a fiesta look, sprinkle the top and sides with 1½ cups crushed Almond Roca or other toffee-type candy.

Makes two (9-inch) layer cakes or one Bundt cake.

1 box devil's food cake mix	4 eggs
2 tablespoons unsweetened cocoa powder	⅓ cup vegetable oil
1 cup water	¼ cup instant espresso powder
½ cup grated bittersweet chocolate	¼ cup Kahlúa
¼ cup cognac	4 teaspoons ground cinnamon

1. Heat oven, prepare pan(s) and mix as in Steps 1 and 2 above.
2. Bake 9-inch layers for 30 minutes or until they spring back when pressed on the sides and in the middle. Bake the Bundt cake for about 45 minutes.
3. Let rest in the pan(s) about 5 minutes before inverting onto a cake rack to cool. Let cool completely before frosting.

Carole's Perfect Brownies

Research tells us fourteen out of any ten individuals likes chocolate.

—Sandra Boynton

Chocolate expert and author Carole Bloom is also a friend. Since no entertaining book would be complete without a perfect brownie, naturally I asked Carole for her recommendation. The brownie she chose as the universal favorite is the very fudgy one below. The simple variations introduce tropical flavors and a white chocolate frosting. This recipe is also the basis for the ice cream sandwiches (page 182).

Kid Appeal • Completed in Advance • Buffet

PARTY TIME PREPARATIONS: **None.**

SERVING EQUIPMENT: **Large platter or basket.**

BEVERAGE TO ACCOMPANY: **Port, Australian Muscat, sweet sherry**

Makes 16 (2-inch) brownies

1 tablespoon butter, softened, for the pan	2 teaspoons pure vanilla extract
4 ounces unsweetened chocolate, finely chopped	½ cup all-purpose flour
3 ounces bittersweet chocolate, finely chopped	2 tablespoons unsweetened Dutch-processed cocoa powder
¾ cup (1½ sticks) butter, cut into small pieces	⅛ teaspoon salt
4 large eggs, room temperature	1 cup walnuts, finely chopped
1¼ cups sugar	

1. Preheat the oven to 350°F (180°C). Line an 8-inch square baking pan with a large piece of aluminum foil, letting it hang over the edges about 2 inches. Butter the foil lightly with the 1 tablespoon butter.

2. Place the unsweetened chocolate, bittersweet chocolate and butter in the top of a double boiler over hot water. (Or combine the chocolates and butter in a microwave-proof bowl and melt in a microwave oven on Low for 30-second bursts). Stir often with a rubber spatula to ensure even melting. Remove the top pan of the double boiler and wipe the bottom and sides very dry. Let stand to cool for 10 minutes, stirring often to prevent a skin from forming on top.

3. Using a mixer, whip the eggs in a large mixing bowl until frothy. Add the sugar and whip until the mixture is very pale and thick and holds a slowly dissolving ribbon

as the beater is lifted. Blend in the vanilla.

4. Sift the flour, cocoa powder and salt onto a piece of waxed paper.

5. Add the melted chocolate mixture to the egg and sugar mixture and blend thoroughly. In three stages, add the flour and cocoa mixture to the batter, blending well after each addition. Stir in the walnuts.

6. Transfer the batter to the prepared baking pan. Bake the brownies for 45 minutes, until a tester inserted in the center comes out with only a few streaky crumbs clinging to it. Remove the pan from the oven and transfer it to a cooling rack to cool completely.

7. To cut the brownies, lift them from the baking pan by holding onto the edges of the aluminum foil and place on a cutting board. Peel the foil away from the sides of the brownies. Cut into 4 rows in each direction, wiping the knife between cuts. Store in an airtight container between layers of waxed paper at room temperature for up to 4 days. Freeze for longer storage.

❦ VARIATIONS

Tropical Rum Brownies Replace the walnuts with ¾ cup chopped cashew nuts. Add ¼ cup shredded coconut and 2 tablespoons dark rum.

Frosted Mocha Brownies Frost the brownies, before cutting, with the Butter Cream Frosting (page 189). A chocolate-covered coffee bean is a nice addition in the center of each slice.

Mocha Ice Cream Sandwiches

Ice cream desserts are a great solution for entertaining. They are typically easy to make and they can be finished and popped into the freezer up to a week before the party. And ice cream ranks first or second on most everyone's list of favorite sweets. Kids think these special ice cream sandwiches are very cool, grown-ups are tickled by the retro presentation and everyone loves the taste.

This recipe includes two very different "sandwich" elements for this groovy dessert. The fudgy brownie, from page 180, is a gourmet version of the chocolate cookie found in traditional sandwiches. I suggest using coffee or almond crunch ice cream, but any premium ice cream that you like in combination with chocolate would be good, too. The variation features a polenta ginger shortbread, which is delicious on its own for a tea party, brunch or picnic and perfect sandwiched with mango, vanilla, coconut or bittersweet chocolate ice cream.

Kid Appeal • Completed in Advance • Casual

PARTY TIME PREPARATIONS: None. This should be finished and in the freezer before the party.

SERVING EQUIPMENT: None.

Makes 9 sandwiches

1 recipe Carole's Perfect Brownies (page 180), sliced according to directions below	9 scoops premium coffee or almond crunch ice cream (about 1 quart)

1. Prepare either the basic brownie or the tropical variation.
2. When cool, cut the brownies in 3 rows in each direction. Then slice each individual brownie in half horizontally.
3. Remove the ice cream to a bowl and let soften at room temperature for 4 to 5 minutes. Place a brownie square, cut side up, on a large sheet of freezer-quality plastic wrap. Put a generous scoop of the softened ice cream on the brownie. Top with the other half of the brownie, and press gently to settle the layers together. Wrap tightly with the plastic wrap and freeze at least one hour to set. For a more dramatic presentation, slice each brownie horizontally into thirds and layer with two scoops of ice cream. The sandwiches can be prepared and held in the freezer for at least one week.
4. TO SERVE: To conclude a casual meal the sandwiches can be presented simply garnished with fresh fruit. For a more formal plate, using the 3-layer sandwich, lay the stack on its side. Dust the sandwich and plate with cocoa powder or drizzle on one

of the fruit sauces on page 186 and put 3 raspberries or 2 slices of peach or a lavender blossom on top of the sandwich.

※ VARIATIONS

Polenta Ginger Cookie Ice Cream Sandwiches
Makes 8 to 9 sandwiches (16 to 18 cookies)

1½ cups all-purpose flour	¼ cup minced crystallized ginger
1 cup coarse cornmeal or polenta	2 tablespoons grated fresh ginger
1 cup sugar	¼ teaspoon almond extract
½ pound (1 cup) unsalted butter, room temperature	4 teaspoons grated lemon zest
2 egg yolks	1 tablespoon cold water, if needed

1. Combine the flour and cornmeal on a sheet of waxed paper.
2. Use an electric mixer to cream the sugar and butter together. Add the egg yolks, both types of ginger, the almond extract and zest and beat briefly to blend. Add the flour mixture and stir to blend. If the dough is crumbly, add cold water, a little at a time, until the dough can be pressed to form a ball.
3. Shape the dough into 2 flat discs. Wrap in plastic wrap and chill for at least 1 hour.
4. Preheat the oven to 375°F (190°C). Put the chilled dough on a lightly floured board, roll out to about ¼-inch thickness and cut into discs with a 3- to 4-inch cookie cutter. Arrange the cookies on a lightly greased cookie sheet, at least 1 inch apart (they will spread).
5. Bake for 12 to 14 minutes, until the edges are golden. Let cool on the baking sheet for 2 to 3 minutes, then transfer to a wire rack to cool.
6. Proceed as above in Step 3 using mango, coconut or French vanilla ice cream and the cookies instead of the brownies for the ice cream sandwiches.

Dessert Sauces

Cardamom-Scented Crème Anglaise

This elegant sauce can be made without the cardamom to produce a silky vanilla sauce for poached fruit, fresh berries or brownies. The variations with ginger and mint replacing the cardamom are delicately enticing sauces, too.

Completed in Advance • Casual • Formal • Buffet

PARTY TIME PREPARATIONS: Heat, if desired, and serve.

SERVING EQUIPMENT: Bowl and dessert spoon.

Makes 2½ cups

1½ teaspoons cardamom seeds	¼ cup sugar
2 cups milk	1 teaspoon vanilla extract
6 egg yolks	

1. Crush the cardamom seeds in a mortar and pestle or with a heavy knife.
2. Combine the milk and cardamom in a saucepan. Bring to a simmer over medium heat. Remove the pan from the heat and let the cardamom steep for 30 minutes. Strain out the cardamom seeds.
3. In a saucepan, beat the egg yolks with the sugar until thick and pale.
4. Gently reheat the milk for 1 to 2 minutes in the microwave until very hot.
5. Slowly add the hot milk, ¼ cup at a time, into the egg mixture, stirring constantly with a wooden spoon or spatula. Cook over low heat until the mixture thickens slightly, enough to coat the back of a spoon. Do not let it boil or the milk will curdle.
6. Remove the pan from the heat and stir in the vanilla. Continue to stir for 1 to 2 minutes to ensure that the cream cools and doesn't keep cooking. Cool the cream at room temperature, then refrigerate for up to 3 days or use immediately.

Vanilla Bean Sauce Replace the cardamom in Step 2 with one vanilla bean sliced lengthwise. After steeping, remove the vanilla bean from the pan and scrape the tiny seeds from each pod back into the milk. Eliminate the vanilla extract in Step 6.

Ginger Cream Sauce In Step 1, replace the cardamom with 2 tablespoons grated or minced fresh ginger.

Mint Cream Sauce In Step 1, replace the cardamom with 2 tablespoons chopped fresh mint that you strain out as for the cardamom. The vanilla in Step 6 can be replaced with 1 teaspoon green or white crème de menthe.

Raspberry Sauce

Fruit sauces are the epitome of simple. Fresh (or thanks to modern freezing techniques, unsweetened frozen) fruit, sugar and maybe a little liqueur are pureed, strained and chilled. My basic recipe is for raspberry, however blueberry, loganberry, black currant or boysenberry can be used with equal success. Serve a pair of these vividly colored sauces, for instance mango and blackberry, side by side over a simple dessert like purchased cheesecake or ice cream to create a beautiful plate.

Makes about 2 cups

4 cups fresh or frozen unsweetened berries (about 18 ounces frozen), drained well if frozen

¼ to ½ cup powdered sugar

1 to 2 tablespoons lemon juice or balsamic vinegar

1 teaspoon grated orange zest

¼ teaspoon freshly grated nutmeg or ground ginger

1. Puree the fruit in a blender. Add the remaining ingredients and blend. Strain the sauce to remove the seeds.

   The sauce can be prepared and stored, refrigerated, for up to 1 week.

❈ VARIATION

Peach or Mango Sauce Substitute fresh or frozen chopped peaches (about 20 ounces frozen) for the raspberries. Use 1 tablespoon lemon juice plus 2 tablespoons amaretto or apricot brandy. Eliminate the nutmeg. Complete as above.

Whipping cream is one of the simplest and most versatile dessert toppings. Cream with a fat content of 30 percent or more can be whipped, but heavy whipping cream with 36 to 40 percent fat will produce a more stable final product and will be less likely to separate or weep when standing. Whipped cream will hold well in the refrigerator for at least an hour.

Cream can be whipped by hand but it's much easier with an electric mixer. Whichever method you select, the cream and all equipment (metal bowl and whisk) must be well chilled. Gently fold flavoring ingredients into the whipped cream after it has been whipped to a soft peak. Powdered sugar adds the most stability to whipped cream, but superfine sugar may also be used. One quart of cream will produce about two quarts of whipped cream.

Whipped cream can be flavored with sugar and ground spices like allspice, anise, cardamom, powdered chocolate, cinnamon, cloves, ginger, mace or nutmeg. Liquid flavorings like extracts of vanilla, almond, coffee or lemon and alcohol like brandy, port, eau de vie or liqueur may be folded into the whipped cream. Fruit purees and zest of lemon or orange may also be folded into the finished whipped cream before serving.

Good flavoring proportions for 1 quart whipping cream (add more to taste): 1 to 2 teaspoons ground spice, 2 teaspoons extract and/or 2 to 3 tablespoons liqueur.

Dark Chocolate Ganache

This very easy frosting re-creates the decadent flavor of a good truffle.

Makes enough to frost a 2-layer cake, about 2½ cups

| 14 ounces bittersweet chocolate | 1½ cups whipping cream |

1. Roughly chop the chocolate and put in the food processor. Pulse briefly to finely chop.
2. Heat the cream in a saucepan just to the boiling point. With the motor running, pour the cream into the chocolate and process to melt/blend together completely.
3. Transfer the ganache to a bowl. If you plan to use it immediately, chill the frosting by placing it over a bowl of ice or let it cool at room temperature. The ganache must be cool, not cold, to be spreadable. Once cooled, the ganache can be whipped

to create a lighter frosting variation. Refrigerate after applying the frosting to the cool cake.

✹ VARIATIONS

Raspberry-Chocolate Ganache Add 1 to 2 tablespoons of framboise (raspberry liqueur) in Step 2.

White-Chocolate Ganache Replace the dark chocolate with 14 ounces chopped white chocolate and reduce the cream to 1 cup plus 1 tablespoon.

White Chocolate–Ginger Ganache Make the White-Chocolate Ganache. Add ⅓ cup minced candied ginger and ½ teaspoon ground ginger in with the cream.

Light Butter Cream Frosting

Replacing some of the butter in a traditional butter cream with cream cheese makes for a lighter, less sweet frosting that my guests prefer. If you want the classic, replace the cream cheese with a second stick of butter.

Makes enough to frost a 2-layer cake, about 2½ cups

1 stick (½ cup) unsalted butter, softened	3 to 4 tablespoons whipping cream
4 ounces cream cheese	1 teaspoon vanilla extract
3½ cups powdered sugar	Pinch salt

1. Use an electric mixer to cream the butter and cream cheese. Gradually work in the sugar and the cream, beating well after each addition.
2. Add remaining ingredients and whip to desired stiffness, 2 to 3 minutes.
3. Refrigerate cake after frosting.

❋ VARIATIONS

Rum Butter Cream Frosting Replace 2 tablespoons of the cream with 2 table-spoons of dark rum plus ½ teaspoon ground ginger.

Bourbon Butter Cream Frosting Replace 2 tablespoons of the cream with 3 tablespoons of bourbon plus ½ teaspoon ground cinnamon and 4 ounces of cream cheese.

Coffee Butter Cream Frosting Replace 2 tablespoons of the cream with ¼ cup Kahlúa plus 2 teaspoons instant powdered espresso and 2 tablespoons butter. Reduce the vanilla to ½ teaspoon.

Cordial Desserts

The following alcoholic concoctions have more to do with a hot fudge sundae than a martini. I like to serve these instead of dessert after a heavy dinner, or alongside a simple fruit dessert.

White Cloud

Makes 8 drinks

1 cup whipping cream

2 teaspoons powdered sugar

3 cups milk

½ cup grated white chocolate

½ teaspoon vanilla extract

1½ cups frangelico

Nutmeg, for grating

1. Whip the cream with the sugar to soft peaks.
2. Put milk in a heavy-bottomed saucepan and heat to just below the boiling point. Skim any foam from the surface.
3. Immediately pour hot milk over grated chocolate and stir to melt chocolate. Add vanilla and frangelico.
4. **TO SERVE:** Ladle about ½ cup into each heat-resistant serving glass (preferably a bolla or snifter) and top with whipped cream and freshly grated nutmeg. For a variation, glaze the rim of the glass with lemon juice and brown sugar.

Bananas Foster Flip

Makes 8 drinks

1 quart softened French vanilla ice cream

2 cups chopped, ripe bananas

½ cup crème de cacao or Godiva liqueur

1 cup dark rum

1½ cups premium vanilla vodka

2 cups chilled cream soda

Unsweetened cocoa powder

1. Puree all ingredients except the cream soda and cocoa powder. Stir in the soda.
2. Pour into tall soda or tulip glasses and garnish with a dusting of cocoa powder. Serve with giant straws.

Cocktail Connection

AN INVITATION TO A COCKTAIL PARTY conjures up sexy images—the clinking of beautiful glasses, women in flirty little dresses, vibrant conversations and the music of conviviality. Great cocktails carry with them an aura of romance and seduction from an era we desperately miss. An era when Audrey Hepburn was the perfect woman and Sean Connery *was* James Bond. When everyone ate red meat, no one ate sprouts and a party was incomplete without martinis and Manhattans. Included in this chapter are some classic cocktails and some current additions of mine to add an aura of romance to your next "cocktail" party.

Evan Lewis, who has cooked with me and tested recipes with me for years, is responsible for some of these cocktails. She is a top-notch mixologist and martini aficionado.

Mojito

This cocktail has been the national drink of Cuba for decades. Its sprightly combination of tons of fresh mint and lime makes it a sensation any time the weather is hot.

Makes 8 cocktails

¾ cup fresh lime juice

1 small bunch mint, washed, dried and chopped (set aside 8 pretty spears)

½ cup sugar

1½ to 2 cups white rum, preferably Bacardi silver

Cracked ice

½ cup club soda

Lime wedges

1. Pour ¼ cup of lime juice into an ice cube tray. Add a perfect small mint leaf to each slot and freeze until hard. Chill a pretty, clear pitcher for at least half an hour.

2. Combine the mint and the sugar in a heavy bowl. Use a wooden spoon to "muddle" them together (use the back of the spoon to crush the mint and the sugar together into a paste). Stir in the remaining lime juice and rum and mix until the sugar is all dissolved.

3. **TO SERVE:** Fill the chilled pitcher with 2 cups cracked ice and pour the cocktail mixture over. Stir briskly with the wooden spoon to mix and chill the liquid. Add the decorated lime cubes. Serve in a highball glass topped with a splash of club soda. Garnish with a mint spear and lime wedge.

Peach Sangria

Peaches are definitely one of everyone's favorite fruits. This easy-to-make peach variation of sangria really gives a picnic or garden party a boost of sunny summer flavor. To serve at a picnic, wait to add the soda until you are ready to enjoy.

Makes 8 tall drinks

2 cups chopped peaches, plus 1 whole peach sliced for garnish

⅔ cup superfine sugar

2 teaspoons grated lemon or orange zest

⅓ cup peach schnapps or peach liqueur

2 (750-ml) bottles of rosé (like Spanish Rosado by Chivite)

2 to 3 cups sparkling water or soda

Lavender or mint to garnish each glass

1. Combine the chopped peaches, sugar and lemon zest and let sit for 1 hour.
2. Combine the macerated peaches, schnapps and rosé in a large (preferably clear) pitcher and stir to blend. Refrigerate for 30 to 60 minutes.
3. **TO SERVE:** Add the soda and stir to blend. Add ice cubes and stir to chill. Serve with a peach slice speared with lavender or mint on the lip of each glass.

✺ VARIATION

Freeze 2 trays of ice cubes with a raspberry or rose petal in each.

Cosmopolitan Sunset

Freezing the rosy cranberry juice into cubes allows you to keep this cocktail cool on the buffet without diluting its potency with plain ice cubes. The cubes also create a pretty "sunset" pattern as they melt. I am a huge fan of pomegranate juice in cooking; if you can find it, I think it's a sophisticated alternative to the cranberry juice.

Makes 6 cocktails

¼ cup cranberry or pomegranate juice

18 ounces (2¼ cups) premium vodka, such as Ketel One or Absolut

3 ounces (6 tablespoons) Rose's lime juice

1½ ounces (3 tablespoons) Cointreau liqueur

Lime slices, for garnish

1. Pour the cranberry or pomegranate juice into an ice cube tray and freeze.
2. Combine the vodka, lime juice and Cointreau in a large bowl. Add 2 to 3 cups of ice and stir briefly to chill, 5 to 10 seconds. Strain into a pretty, clear pitcher. Chill for at least half an hour. Chill 6 martini glasses.
3. **TO SERVE:** Garnish each glass with a wheel of sliced lime. If you are going to serve everyone immediately, put 1 or 2 cranberry cubes in the bottom of each glass and pour the vodka blend over it. If you want this to sit out on the buffet for a few minutes, add the cranberry cubes to the pitcher and allow guests to serve themselves in the chilled, garnished glasses.

Gingerita

The margarita has been a popular cocktail for so long, and I was thrilled when we came up with this zippy variation on the classic. The fresh ginger juice in the cocktail goes beautifully with the lime juice and tequila. This cocktail really elicits a wow from guests. And as a friend of mine laughingly suggested, all of that ginger would probably settle an upset stomach, too.

This is best served in a pitcher over ice with the handsomely garnished glasses and a bucket of crushed ice on the side for guests to make their own. If you like, leave the tequila out of the mix and serve on the side for guests to add to their liking.

Make 8 cocktails

½ cup minced, peeled fresh ginger

2 tablespoons sugar

1 cup (8 ounces) fresh lime juice

½ cup (4 ounces) triple sec

2 cups (16 ounces) good tequila, such as Commemerativo or Hornitos

For the glass rim: 1 tablespoon sugar well blended with ¼ teaspoon ground ginger in a flat saucer

Lime wedges

1. Puree the fresh ginger in a food processor or mortar and pestle. Put the ginger in a small bowl and pour over 3 tablespoons boiling water. Let steep until cool, then strain through cheesecloth, squeezing and twisting to get all of the liquid. Add sugar and stir to melt. This can be done up to 24 hours ahead.

2. Combine the lime juice, triple sec, ginger syrup and tequila in a pitcher and stir well to blend. Chill for at least 30 minutes.

3. **TO SERVE:** Prepare the traditional rimmed margarita glass (with a twist) by rubbing a lime wedge around the lip of each glass to moisten. Press the rim of the glass firmly into the saucer of ginger sugar. Garnish with a lime wedge.

Mango Champagne Aperitif

This is my contribution to the Bellini cocktail genre: good champagne complemented with a splash of pureed fruit. The floral taste of mango is perfect with dry champagne, and the slightly sweet Muscato completes the delicate fruity flavor of this refreshing aperitif. This is perfect before a luncheon on the terrace or for a Mother's Day brunch.

Make 8 cocktails

½ pound frozen mango chunks

2 to 3 tablespoons sugar

½ cup Muscato

1 (750-ml) bottle chilled dry champagne

4 to 5 lavender blossoms or rose petals, chopped

1. Combine the mango and sugar in a blender and pulse to puree. Add the Muscato and blend briefly.

2. **TO SERVE:** Fill a chilled champagne flute halfway with the mango-Muscato combination. Add chilled champagne to fill and stir gently to blend. Sprinkle with chopped lavender blossom.

Martini Madness

*The fretful neurotic who shakes up an after work martini should emerge
from the experience a changed human being: more generous and sociable,
inclined toward deeper thought and the pleasures of the imagination.*

—William Grimes, "Straight Up on the Rocks"

Stirred or shaken, served with an olive, a "firecracker" or a twist, martinis are a hit with the party crowd. Purists and others with adamant opinions on the perfect martini abound, so be forewarned before you attempt this cocktail. Following are some fun variations and the Classic Atomizer Dry Martini, a selection sure to please everyone.

To prepare for a great martini, have on hand a cocktail shaker (preferably metal) and the classic stemmed glass. The glasses should be well chilled ahead of time in the refrigerator or freezer.

Classic Atomizer Dry Martini with "Firecrackers"

Let's get out of these wet clothes and into a dry martini.

—Robert Benchley

This is the martini for the person who can never get theirs "dry" enough. If you have a vermouth atomizer, specifically sold for this purpose, use that to introduce a mist of vermouth to each cocktail before adding the chilled gin.

Makes 4 drinks

1 to 2 teaspoons dry vermouth

2 cups ice

12 to 16 ounces premium gin, such as
Bombay Sapphire

8 large green "firecracker" olives stuffed with
jalapeño chile

1. If you have a vermouth atomizer, mist the inside of each glass with vermouth. Otherwise, add the 1 teaspoon of vermouth to the first chilled glass. Swirl to coat the inside, then pour that into the second glass and so on. After you have coated all 4 glasses in this way, discard any remaining vermouth. Drop a stuffed olive in the bottom of each glass.

2. Put the ice into your metal cocktail shaker and shake for 10 seconds. The shaker should feel icy. Add the gin and shake to chill for 15 seconds. Strain the very cold gin into the prepared glasses.

Appletini

This is a beautiful green color and very appealing to those preferring something "lighter."

Makes 2 drinks

1 tablespoon sugar mixed with ¼ teaspoon ground cinnamon

2 cups ice

¾ cup premium vodka, like Ketel One or Absolut

½ cup sour apple schnapps

1. Moisten the rim of each chilled glass and press into the sugar mixture.
2. Put the cracked ice into your metal cocktail shaker and shake for 10 seconds. The shaker should feel icy. Add the vodka and schnapps and shake to chill for 15 seconds.
3. Strain the very cold liquid into the prepared glasses.

Grandma's Cookie

This cocktail is an uncanny duplication of the taste of an oatmeal cookie.

Makes 4 drinks

1 tablespoon sugar mixed with ⅛ teaspoon ground nutmeg

2 cups ice

¾ cup premium vodka

¾ cup frangelico

1. Moisten the rim of each chilled glass and press into the sugar mixture.
2. Put the ice into your metal cocktail shaker and shake for 10 seconds. The shaker should feel icy. Add the vodka and frangelico and shake to chill for 15 seconds.
3. Strain the very cold liquid into the prepared glasses.

Chocolate Martini

Makes 4 drinks

2 ounces dark or milk chocolate

2 cups ice

12 ounces Stoli Vanilla vodka

6 ounces white crème de cacao

Orange peel strip

1. Melt the chocolate on a saucer in the microwave. To coat the glass rims with chocolate, holding each glass by the base, dip the rim of the glass into the melted chocolate and twirl the stem. This will create an appealing, free-form chocolate coating around the lip of the glass.
2. Put the ice into your metal cocktail shaker and shake for 10 seconds. The shaker should feel icy. Add the vodka and crème de cacao and shake to chill for 15 seconds.
3. Strain the very cold liquid into martini glasses. Garnish with an orange peel strip.

Menus: Occasions for Entertaining

I OPENED MY FIRST CATERING business when I was thirteen. Seriously. No one in our small town wanted to hire a thirteen year old and I was determined to earn enough money to go to Europe when I turned eighteen. I canvassed my neighborhood, knocking at Mrs. McGuire's, at Bev and Kathy's next door, the Williams's and the French's. I made them all what turned out to be an irresistible offer: for $5 I would shop for, prepare and serve a "gourmet" dinner to them one night a week. I signed up seven families and then confessed to my parents what I was up to. I had to; I needed my mother to take me to the grocery store to shop for my "engagements."

I had two cookbooks from which to draw inspiration for this new business: my only cookbook, Betty Crocker's *Cooking For Kids*, and my mother's untouched *Larousse Gastronomique*. These disparate resources resulted in some extraordinary menus: canard a l'orange followed by s'mores was such a hit I served it to every house on my

route. Crêpe Suzettes, which I saw as the acme of French sophistication, were a blazing success, even when I caught the McGuire's heirloom tablecloth on fire. When I became confident enough to invent a dish, I promoted pigs in a blanket from hors d'oeuvres to entrée and completed that menu with an elegant chocolate soufflé (I've never made its equal since).

Over the years my menus have become more cohesive and less likely to cause gastric confusion. However, I'm sure I've never regained the unselfconscious zeal I felt at thirteen when first given license to plan a "party."

The following section features my menu solutions to nearly every type of party your year might hold. Notice that all of the menus are completed with recipes contained in this book plus purchased additions. The menus are meant to provide a balance of texture, flavor and style and be appropriate to the season and the occasion. You could purchase any of the elements for which a recipe is provided or replace a suggested clam chowder with your own lobster stew and still reap the benefits of the overall plan.

Menus: Year-Round Entertaining for 2 to 24

January

New Year's Day Open House: Red-Eye Brunch for 24

Coffee station with brandy and whipped cream
Albacore Gravlax Platter (page 20) with Ginger-Wasabi Sauce (page 21) and pickled ginger
Tarte Pissaladiere (page 31)
Olives and nuts

Spinach and Pomegranate Salad (page 51) with Evan's Tangerine Vinaigrette (page 135)
Arugula Pesto Roast Lamb (page 81, 138)
Grilled Vegetables (page 69)
Pita breads

White Chocolate–Banana-Coconut Cheesecake (page 165)
Chocolate dessert (purchased)

Super Bowl: The Chili Bowl Snack Party for 8

Party Nuts (two types; page 43 or purchased)
Grilled Chicken Skewers (see page 4) with Cilantro Pesto (page 138)
Cheese board (see page 29)
Avocado-Chipotle Salsa (page 144) with chips
Southwest Caesar Salad (page 51)
Mole Poblano–Style Chili with Beans (page 103)
Cornbread muffins (purchased)
Beer

Carole's Perfect Brownies (page 180)
Fruit tart (purchased)

Skiing Adventure: Snowman Picnic for 8

Hot toddies

Crudité with Provençal Olive and Citrus Dip (page 38)
Classic Swiss Fondue (page 27) with French bread and green apples

New England Clam Chowder with Bacon (page 108)
Dinner rolls (purchased)

Coconut-Ginger Risotto Dolce (page 170)

40th Birthday: Special Dinner Party for 8

Boiled Shrimp with Rouille (page 140)
Mushroom and Artichoke Heart Dip (page 36) with French bread
Chicken Liver Porcini Pâté (page 25) with Crostini (page 16)

Crab Cakes (page 6)

Roast Chicken with Shiitake Mushrooms (page 93)
Golden Mashed Potatoes (page 63)
Steamed green beans and cherry tomatoes (see page 67) with Tarragon Butter (page 145)

Pouilly-Fumè

Mexican Chocolate Crème Brûlée (page 159)
Coffee

February

There is no sincerer love than the love of food.
—George Bernard Shaw

Valentine's Day: Dinner for 2

Oysters on the Half Shell with Evan's Tangerine Vinaigrette (page 135)
Champagne

Stuffed Mushrooms (page 11)

Individual Beef and Gorgonzola Wellingtons (page 80)
Oven-roasted red peppers and asparagus (see page 56)
Bordeaux

Polenta Ginger Cookie Ice Cream Sandwiches (cookies cut into heart shapes; page 183)
or purchased dessert
Coffee

8th Birthday Lunch: Buffet for 16 (children and their parents)

Lemonade and beer
Assorted Party Pinwheels (page 42)
Tortilla chips and Salsa Rustica without chiles (page 141)
Tropical Fiesta Salad (page 53)
Beef and Turkey Burgers (pages 111–113) with all of the fixings
(or you may purchase pizza for the children)
Potato chips

Sharon's Orange Blossom Cake (page 175) with Dark Chocolate Ganache (page 187)
Vanilla ice cream

10th Anniversary Buffet Supper for 24

Brie en Croûte with Chèvre and Mushrooms (page 23)
Thai Crab Cakes (page 7) or purchased crab cakes
Grilled Vegetable Platter with Mediterranean Sesame-Oregano Dip (page 40)
Pear, Gorgonzola and Arugula Salad with Sherry Vinaigrette (page 51)
Pork Tenderloin with Balsamic Blueberry Sauce (page 77)
Swordfish Souvlaki (page 98)

Pumpkin Polenta with Pecans (page 55)
Focaccia (purchased)

Alsatian Riesling

White Chocolate–Lemon Cloud (page 168)
Napoleons (purchased)
Coffee

March

Only Irish coffee provides in a single glass all four essential food
groups: alcohol, caffeine, sugar and fat.

—Alex Levine

St. Patrick's Day Supper for 8

Guinness Stout
Goat Cheese and Sun-Dried Tomato Pizzettes (page 4)
Pesto Crostini (page 17) with purchased smoked salmon, capers, lemon and minced onion
Braised-Beef Short Ribs with Mushroom-Thyme Sauce (page 84)
Golden Mashed Potatoes (page 63)
Oven-roasted leeks (page 58)

Trifle (purchased) topped with a drizzle of Bailey's Cream
Irish coffee

Baby Shower: Casual Luncheon for 8

Tartlets with Goat Cheese and Arugula Pesto (page 9)
Crudités with Sun-Dried Tomato Spread (page 40)
Ruby Fruit Salad (page 53)
Shiitake Mushroom and Brie Strata (page 102)

Carole's Perfect Brownies (page 180)

Mango iced tea

Oscar Party: Casual TV Dinner for 8

Snow crab claws (purchased) with Lemon Parmesan Aïoli (page 139)
Spiced Nuts (page 44)

Italian Fontina Fondue (page 28) with fennel, focaccia and sausage for dipping

Individual Chicken Pot Pies (page 95)
Baby Greens with Herbs, Walnuts and Feta (page 51)

Chardonnay

Espresso Crème Brûlée with a twist of lemon (page 159) or purchased dessert
Coffee

April

My doctor told me to stop having intimate dinners for four.
Unless there are three other people.

—Orson Welles

Elegant 50th Birthday for 8

Spicy Tangerine Shrimp (page 3)
Oysters on the half shell
Champagne
Portobello Mushrooms Stuffed with Bacon and Sage (page 13)

Roast Tenderloin of Beef with Horseradish-Dijon Butter (page 74)
Oven-roasted zucchini with thyme and asiago (see page 57)
Wasabi Mashed Potatoes (page 64)

Cabernet Sauvignon

Black and White Chocolate Terrine (page 154) with Raspberry Sauce (page 186)
Coffee

Easter Luncheon Buffet for 16

Cooked shrimp and crab claws (purchased) with Rouille Sauce (page 140)

Endive, butter lettuce, strawberry and Brie salad with Evan's Tangerine Vinaigrette (page 135)
Cedar-Planked Salmon (page 106)
Festival Sweet Potato and Leek Gratin (page 59)
Steamed asparagus (page 67) with Basil Butter (page 145)

Sparkling apple juice
Prosecco

Coconut-Macadamia Cake (page 176) with Rum Butter Cream Frosting (page 189)

May

Kentucky Derby Brunch for 8

Mint julep or Mojito (page 192)

Mini Brie en Croûte with Pecan Praline and Apricots (page 23)

Mushroom Salad with Tahini-Lemon Vinaigrette (page 134)
Shrimp with Vodka Tomato Sauce on fusilli pasta (page 118)
Steamed asparagus (page 67) with Lemon Butter (page 145)

Pastries (purchased)
Crepes (page 161) with fresh strawberries and basil (page 161)

Coffee and iced tea

Mother's Day Brunch for 8

Mango Champagne Aperitif (page 196)
Lemon-Basil Crostini (page 16) with feta and honey

Italian Essentials Strata (page 102)
Cointreau Kiwifruit Salad (page 53)
Grilled asparagus, radicchio and cherry tomatoes (see page 69)

Italian rolls (purchased)

Nectarine Amaretto Cheesecake (page 165)
Coffee

College Graduation Celebration: Buffet for 24

Hot Scampi Dip (page 35) with crusty bread
Goat Cheese and Sun-Dried Tomato Pizzettes (page 4)
Tortilla chips and Mango Salsa (page 144) or purchased
Raspberry Kumquat Salad (page 53)
Chicken Curry (page 90) with all of the condiments
Grilled vegetable skewers composed of eggplant, mushrooms and cherry tomatoes (see page 69)
Jasmine rice (page 62)
India pale ale and lassi

White Chocolate –Banana-Coconut Cheesecake (page 165) or purchased Indian dessert
Coffee

Wedding Engagement Party: Buffet Dinner for 16

Candied Nuts (page 43)
Sausage Mushrooms (see page 11)
Tarte Pissaladiere (page 31)
Pâté (purchased) with crackers

Baby Greens with Herbs, Walnuts and Feta (page 51)
Quintessential Herb Roasted Chicken (page 92)
Goat Cheese Mashed Potatoes (page 64)
Oven-roasted carrots, red onion and leeks (see page 57)
Cedar-Planked Salmon (page 106)

Pinot Noir, Sauvignon Blanc

Fig and Mascarpone Risotto Dolce (page 170)
Coffee

Memorial Day Barbecue for 16

Balsamic Cheese Nibbles (page 5)
Mango Salsa (page 144) on chèvre with tortilla chips
Deviled Eggs (page 4) with Sesame-Ginger Mayonnaise (page 140)

Lamb Shashlik (page 97) and Swordfish Souvlaki (page 98)
Nicole's Tabbouleh (page 53)
Raspberry Kumquat Salad (page 53)

Beaujolais and Viognier

Frosted Mocha Brownies (page 181)
Polenta Ginger Cookies (page 183)
Fresh fruit
Coffee

Cinco de Mayo

Gingeritas (page 195) or margaritas
El Paso Fondue (page 28) drizzled over a platter of corn chips, sliced avocado and cooked shrimp
Guacamole (purchased)

Frijoles Ranchero (page 65)
Oven-roasted Spanish onions and red bell peppers (see page 57)
Pork Tenderloin with Fig Sauce (page 76)
Purchased tortillas

Mexican Chocolate Cake (page 179) or purchased flan
Coffee

June

**Reminds me of my safari in Africa. Somebody forgot the corkscrew
and for several days we had to live on nothing but food and water.**

—W. C. Fields

30th Birthday Picnic for 16
Peach Sangria (page 193)

Pesto Crostini (page 17) with tomato and feta
Smoked Salmon Potato Salad (page 52)
Paris Bistro Salad (page 51)
Green Grape and Chicken Tortellini Salad (page 52)
Party Pinwheels with chèvre, bacon and tomato (see page 42)

Almond-Amontillado Cupcakes (page 176) with Dark Chocolate Ganache (page 187)

Father's Day Dinner for 8
Spicy Tangerine Shrimp (page 3)

New Wave Spinach and Pomegranate Salad (page 51)

Grilled New York Steak with Gorgonzola Cream Sauce (page 146)
Polenta with Wild Mushrooms and Walnuts (page 54)
Steamed green beans (see page 67)

Cabernet Sauvignon

White Chocolate–Banana-Coconut Cheesecake (page 165)
Coffee

Garden Cocktail Party for 16
Anchovy-Less Tarte Pissaladiere (page 32)
Grilled asparagus (page 69) with Lavender Mayonnaise (page 140)
Lamb Shashlik (appetizer size) (page 97)

Cheese board (see page 29)
Lemon-Basil Crostini (page 16) with fresh tomato and basil
Gravlax (page 19) with condiments
Fresh fruit platter

Martini bar (page 197)

July

Thanksgiving is America's national chow-down feast, the one occasion each year when gluttony becomes a patriotic duty (in France, by contrast, there are three such days: Hier, Aujour d'hui and Demain).
—Michael Dresser

Fourth of July Backyard Barbecue for 16
Mojitos (page 192)

Polenta Cups with Grilled Shrimp and Avocado Salsa filling (page 15)
Roasted Eggplant Spread (page 39) with pita chips
Crudité with Mediterranean Sesame-Oregano Dip (page 40)

Cedar-Planked Salmon (page 106)
Asparagus Niçoise (page 50)
Grilled Corn on the Cob (page 60)

Riesling

Blueberries, strawberries, raspberries and Grand Marnier whipped cream or
Rustic Plum-Blackberry Tart (page 173)

Bastille Day Garden Party for 8
French charcuterie including purchased French sausage, French cheeses, French pâté and cornichons, French mustard, French bread and fresh fruit

Blackberries, Pine Nuts and Brie Salad (page 51)
Paris Bistro Salad (page 51) with poached chicken with Sherry Vinaigrette (page 133)
Provençal Fennel Salad (page 51)

Selection of French wines (Chablis, Chenin Blanc, Sauvignon Blanc, Pouilly-Fuisse, Beaujolais)

Crème Brûlée (page 158) with berries
Coffee

August

Beach Party for 8

Mojitos (page 192)

Boiled shrimp with Rouille Sauce (page 140)
Chips with Avocado-Chipotle Salsa (page 144)

Provençal Fennel Salad (page 51) or purchased coleslaw
Basil New Potato Salad (page 52)
Filet mignon sandwich on focaccia with purchased horseradish sauce

Blueberry-Lemon Tart (page 168)

Dinner in the Garden for 8

Grilled lamb skewers (appetizer size) with Arugula Pesto (page 138)
Feta and Honey Wheels (page 4)

Blackberries, Pine Nuts and Brie Salad (page 51)
Salmon with Spinach and Feta in Puff Pastry (page 79)
Steamed sugar snap peas (see page 67) with Ginger Butter (page 145)
Wasabi Mashed Potatoes (page 64)

Riesling

Risotto Dolce Scented with Cardamom and Orange (page 169)
Coffee

September

Housewarming Party: Finger Food for 24

Cosmopolitan Sunsets (page 194)

Gravlax (page 19) or purchased smoked salmon
Curry Spiced Nuts (page 45)
Spanakopita (purchased)
Hot Scampi Dip (page 35) with sourdough bread and green apples
Grilled vegetables (see page 69) with Provençal Olive and Citrus Dip (page 38)
and Sun-Dried Tomato Spread (page 40)
Chicken Liver Porcini Pâté (page 25) with crackers

Polenta Ginger Cookies (page 183) or purchased cookies
Frosted Mocha Brownies (page 181) or purchased truffles
Bowl of berries
Coffee

Labor Day Barbecue for 8

Mojitos (page 192) and beer

Chips
Polenta Cups (page 14) with Warm Teleme and Olive Filling

Southwest Caesar Salad (page 51)
Frijoles Ranchero (page 65)
Grilled corn on the cob (page 60)
Turkey Burgers (page 113) and purchased artisan sausages on the grill

Rustic Plum-Blackberry Tart (page 173) or purchased fruit dessert

Football Homecoming Tailgate Picnic for 8

Coconut-Crab Dip (page 39) with crusty bread
Provençal Fennel Salad (page 51)

Five Sea Creature Stew (Cioppino) (page 86)
Garlic bread

Pinot Noir

Orange–Ginger Tart (page 168)
Biscotti (purchased)
Coffee

October

Laughter is brightest where food is best.
—Irish Proverb

Halloween Buffet Supper for 16

Hot cider spiked with brandy

Crudité with Roasted Eggplant Spread (page 39)

*Lemon-Basil Crostini (page 17) with Smoked Trout Pâté (page 26) or purchased
Goat Cheese and Sun-Dried Tomato Pizzettes (page 4)*

*New Wave Spinach and Pomegranate Salad (page 51)
Pumpkin Polenta with Pecans (page 55)
Cuban-Flavored Braised Beef Short Ribs (page 85)
Garlic bread*

*Rustic Apple-Cranberry Tart (page 172), decorated with pastry spider web and plastic spiders
Halloween candy
Coffee*

Fall Foliage–Watching Picnic for 8

*Cheese and fruit from hors d'oeuvre suggestions
Grilled vegetable antipasto with Tahini-Lemon Vinaigrette (page 134)*

*Thermos of Smoked Fish Chowder (page 109)
Sourdough or corn bread*

Viognier

*Carole's Perfect Brownies (page 180) or purchased apple tart
Coffee*

November

25th Anniversary Dinner Party for 24

Mango Champagne Aperitif (page 196)

*Thai Crab Cakes (page 7) with Herb Sauce (page 6)
Spiced Nuts (page 44)
Olives*

*Pear, Gorgonzola and Arugula Salad (page 51)
Top sirloin roast (chart, page 124)
Sicilian-Style Potato with Fennel Gratin (page 59)
Grilled portobello mushrooms (see page 69)*

Merlot

*Gingered White Chocolate Terrine (page 156)
Coffee*

Traditional Thanksgiving Dinner for 16

Champagne

Gingery Waldorf Salad (page 53)
Roasted Beet and Blue Cheese Salad (page 52)

Roast turkey with your favorite stuffing (chart, page 122)
Festival Sweet Potato and Leek Gratin (page 59)
Oven-roasted zucchini and cherry tomatoes with Asiago cheese (see page 57)
Cranberry sauce (purchased or contributed by guests)

Viognier

Rustic Apple-Cranberry Tart (page 172) with rum whipped cream
Assorted pies (purchased or guest-contributed)
Coffee

Post-Thanksgiving Dinner and Movie
(casual for those in from out of town for Thanksgiving) for 8

Assorted Mexican beers

Celery, jicama, radish, cherry tomatoes with imported olives

Southwest Caesar Salad (page 51)
Mole Poblano–Style Chili with Beans (page 103)
Warm corn tortillas

Leftover pie
Fresh fruit
Coffee

December

Christmas Eve Supper: Casual Buffet for 8

Grandma's Cookie cocktail (page 198)

Nuts, Olives
Crudité with Provençal Olive and Citrus Dip (page 38)

Christmas Salad (page 50)
Braised Beef Short Ribs with Mushroom-Thyme Sauce (page 84)

Polenta with Wild Mushrooms and Walnuts (page 54)

Cabernet Sauvignon

Ice cream with hot fudge sauce and Christmas cookies
Coffee

Holiday Dessert Open House for 24

Classic Swiss Fondue (page 27) with green apples, fennel and French bread cubes
Dessert Crepes (page 161)
Rustic Apple-Cranberry Tart (page 172)
Lemon Amaretto Cheesecake (page 164)
Coconut-Ginger Risotto Dolce (page 170)
Black and White Chocolate Terrine (page 154)

Purchased Christmas cookies, truffles and gingerbread

Grandma's Cookie cocktail (page 198)
Hot spiced cider
Champagne

Chanukah Dinner for 16

Chicken Liver Porcini Pâté (page 25) or purchased and crackers
Latkes (purchased) or Gruyère Walnut Crisps (page 4)
Baby Greens with Herbs, Walnuts and Feta (page 51)

Steamed baby carrots with caraway and honey (page 67)
Couscous with Pistachios (page 61)
Roast Chicken with Tahini (page 93)
Marinated tri-tip roast (chart, page 124)

Chardonnay and Merlot

Rustic Pear-Ginger Tart (page 173) or purchased holiday dessert
Coffee

Christmas Breakfast for 8

Fresh fruit with Vanilla Bean Sauce (page 185)

Strata Vermont (page 101)
Croissants (purchased)

Coffee or hot chocolate with cinnamon whipped cream

Elegant New Year's Eve Supper for 8

Champagne

Caviar Display (see page 37)
Candied Nuts (page 43)
Tartlet with goat cheese, candied ginger, fig and honey (page 9)

Smoked Fish Chowder (page 109)

Roast rack of lamb with rosemary and garlic (chart, page 125)
Wasabi Mashed Potatoes (page 64)
Steamed baby carrots (see page 67) with chives and Orange Butter (page 145)
Cabernet Sauvignon

Candy Bar Blast Chocolate Terrine (page 156)
Port

Index